W9-BRN-474

Boston
day BY day

1st Edition

by Marie Morris

BICENTENNIAL
1807
WILEY
2007
BICENTENNIAL

Wiley Publishing, Inc.

Contents

A Note from the Publisher

Organizing your time. That's what this guide is all about.

Other guides give you long lists of things to see and do and then expect you to fit the pieces together. The Day by Day guides are different. They tell you the best of everything, and then show you how to see it *in the smartest, most time-efficient way*. Our authors have designed detailed itineraries for you, organized by time, neighborhood, or special interest. Each tour comes with a bulleted map that takes you from stop to stop.

Hoping to follow in the footsteps of America's founding fathers, or see the highlights of the Museum of Fine Arts? Planning a walk along the Esplanade, or a whirlwind tour of the very best that Boston has to offer? Whatever your interest or schedule, the Day by Days give you the smartest route to follow. Not only do we take you to the top sights and attractions, but we introduce you to those special moments that only locals know about—those "finds" that turn tourists into travelers.

The Day by Days are also your top choice if you're looking for one complete guide for all your travel needs. The best hotels and restaurants for every budget, the greatest shopping values, the wildest nightlife—it's all here.

Why should you trust our judgment? Because our authors personally visit each place they write about. They're an independent lot who say what they think and would never include places they wouldn't recommend to their best friends. They're also open to suggestions from readers. If you'd like to contact them, please send your comments my way at mspring@wiley.com, and I'll pass them on.

Enjoy your Day by Day guide—the most helpful travel companion you can buy. And have the trip of a lifetime.

Warm regards,

Michael Spring
Publisher
Frommer's Travel Guides

About the Author

Marie Morris grew up in New York and graduated from Harvard, where she studied history. She lives in Boston and has worked for the *Boston Herald, Boston* magazine, and the *New York Times*. She's the author of *Boston For Dummies, Irreverent Guide to Boston,* and she covers Boston for *Frommer's New England*.

An Additional Note

Please be advised that travel information is subject to change at any time—and this is especially true of prices. We therefore suggest that you write or call ahead for confirmation when making your travel plans. The authors, editors, and publisher cannot be held responsible for the experiences of readers while traveling. Your safety is important to us, however, so we encourage you to stay alert and be aware of your surroundings.

Star Ratings, Icons & Abbreviations

Every hotel, restaurant, and attraction listing in this guide has been ranked for quality, value, service, amenities, and special features using a **star-rating system.** Hotels, restaurants, attractions, shopping, and nightlife are rated on a scale of zero stars (recommended) to three stars (exceptional). In addition to the star-rating system, we also use a **kids icon** to point out the best bets for families. Within each tour, we recommend cafes, bars or restaurants where you can take a break. Each of these stops appears in a shaded box marked with a coffee cup–shaped bullet 🍵 .

The following **abbreviations** are used for credit cards:

AE	American Express	DISC	Discover	V	Visa
DC	Diners Club	MC	MasterCard		

Frommers.com

Now that you have the guidebook to a great trip, visit our website at **www. frommers.com** for travel information on more than 3,000 destinations. With features updated regularly, we give you instant access to the most current trip-planning information available. At Frommers.com, you'll also find the best prices on airfares, accommodations, and car rentals—and you can even book travel online through our travel booking partners.

A Note on Prices

In the Take a Break and Best Bets section of this book, we have used a system of dollar signs to show a range of costs for one night in a hotel (the price of a double-occupancy room) or the cost of an entrée at a restaurant. Use the following table to decipher the dollar signs:

Cost	Hotels	Restaurants
$	under $100	under $10
$$	$100–$200	$10–$20
$$$	$200–$300	$20–$30
$$$$	$300–$400	$30–$40
$$$$$	over $400	over $40

An Invitation to the Reader

In researching this book, we discovered many wonderful places—hotels, restaurants, shops, and more. We're sure you'll find others. Please tell us about them, so we can share the information with your fellow travelers in upcoming editions. If you were disappointed with a recommendation, we'd love to know that, too. Please write to:

Frommer's Boston Day by Day, 1st Edition
Wiley Publishing, Inc. • 111 River St. • Hoboken, NJ 07030-5774

14 Favorite
Moments

14 Favorite **Moments**

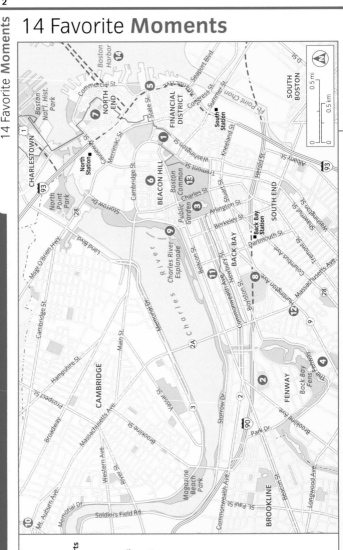

Once in a while, just for a moment, I get a new perspective on my adopted hometown. The sun emerges from a cloud, making the harbor glow. I can't take my eyes off the lush green of the Fenway Park outfield or the sapphire blue of the Charles River. In the Public Garden, a delighted child's laughter rings out. The familiar feels new, and I realize yet again what an endlessly fascinating city Boston is. I'd love to help you find some serendipitous moments of your own. Let's look around.

1 Treading in the footsteps of the Founding Fathers. Only a handful of American cities have histories as rich and varied as Boston's. A walk along the Freedom Trail will cover the highlights. *See p 42.*

2 Feeling like a kid again at Fenway Park. Whether you're a lifelong fan or you've never been to a game before, the oldest park in the major leagues will get to you. Come to a game and cheer on the Little Leaguer next to you waiting to catch a pop-up. *See p 24.*

3 Savoring spring in the Public Garden. Boston's loveliest park is gorgeous year-round, but there's something special about the atmosphere when the bitter New England winter finally recedes. Maybe it's the sheer beauty of the beds of tulips. Or maybe it's just that the pasty-white Bostonians all seem so excited about the change of seasons. *See p 90.*

4 Seeing old friends at the Museum of Fine Arts. Strolling through the MFA, you may find greetings forming on your lips. Hello, Degas dancer. How's everything, Vincent van Gogh? Are your teeth bothering you, President Washington? They may not be the most valuable or significant of the museum's holdings, but the most familiar ones feel like home. *See p 26.*

5 Devouring a lobster. It doesn't matter how much I rave about a stylish bistro or some unusual ethnic cuisine—my out-of-town visitors want seafood, preferably of the bright-red variety. I can't complain—Legal Sea Foods, here we come. *See p 109.*

A young fan takes in a game.

6 Imagining yourself as an American aristocrat. Picturesque Beacon Hill has been a blueblood bastion for almost 400 years. Visitors stroll the cobblestone streets and whisper: "This is exactly what I thought Boston would look like." *See p 46.*

7 Savoring a taste of Italy. Rush, rush, rush. Sightsee, photograph. Wait—what's this? A caffè that serves perfect espresso? Is this the North End we've been hearing so much about? Why, yes, we really could use a break. A cappuccino would be lovely, thanks. *See p 50.*

8 Riding on the back of a Duck (Tour). My favorite tour is amphibious and unforgettable: It trundles around the city streets before slipping into the placid waters of the Charles River basin. *See p 14.*

9 Wishing the United States a happy birthday. You may think your town makes a big deal about the 4th of July. We celebrate for a week. Boston Harborfest is a citywide event that culminates in a free outdoor concert by the Boston Pops. Hundreds of thousands of people attend. *See p 161.*

10 Channeling a college student. Skip the body art and ill-fitting pants and head to Harvard Square, the heart of a city that's also an age-old, cutting-edge college town. Beyond the brick walls and wrought-iron gates of Harvard Yard is a festival of trendy shopping, gourmet ice cream (maybe *that* explains the baggy pants), and alfresco music. *See p 60.*

11 Wearing the numbers right off your credit cards. Boston offers unique merchandise of all descriptions at all price points. Begin with an inspirational stroll along Newbury Street. *See p 32.*

12 Tapping your foot in time to the music. From the world-famous Boston Symphony Orchestra to the noisiest street corners, Boston's live-music scene creates a unique soundtrack. We must be spoiled, because we take it for granted. *See p 127.*

13 Oohing and ahhing over fireworks. The best night of the year for pyro (technic) maniacs is New Year's Eve, when fireworks explode over Boston Common at 7pm and over Boston Harbor at the stroke of midnight. *See p 162.*

14 Breathing sea breezes on a stuffy day. When summer bears down on the city, a ride across breezy Boston Harbor (for as little as $1.50) grants an interlude, however brief, of wind in your hair and the promise of fall. *See p 9.* ●

The deep, sheltered harbor helped Colonial Boston rise to prominence.

The Best **in One Day**

CHARLESTOWN NAVY YARD

Pier 4

New Rutherford Ave · City Square · Chelsea St · CHARLESTOWN

Paul Revere Park

Inner Harbor

Fiskes Wharf

CHARLESTOWN BR.

93

Revere Plaza

Constitution Wharf

Nashua St

Langone Park

Commercial St

Copp's Hill Burying Ground

Charter St

Battery Wharf

Lomasney Wy

Snowhill St

Sheafe St

Prince St

Tileston St

Lincoln Wharf

North Station

Haverhill St

Endicott St

N Margin St

Salem St

Hanover St

NORTH END

North St

Fleet St

Moon St

Lewis St

Union Wharf

Sargents Wharf

Causeway St · Friend St · Canal St

Portland St · Valenti Wy

Merrimac St

Richmond St

Fulton St

Commercial St

Lewis Wharf

Haymarket

N Washington St

New Sudbury St

Hanover St

Cross St

North St

Atlantic Ave.

Commercial Wharf

Stanniford St

New Chardon St · Bullfinch Pl

Congress St

Surface Rd

Christopher Columbus Park

Cambridge St

Bowdoin

CITY HALL PLAZA

North St

Long Wharf

Russell St · Joy St · Hancock St · Temple St

Bowdoin St

Somerset St

Government Center

State St

Aquarium

Central Wharf

Myrtle St

BEACON HILL

Court St

7 State

Central St

Milk St

India St

India Wharf

3

Beacon St

Park St

School St

Water St

Kilby St

Broad St

Rowes Wharf

2 **4** Bromfield St

Park Street

Pearl St

Oliver St

High St

Post Office Square

NORTHERN AVE. BR. (pedestrian)

BOSTON COMMON

1

Downtown Crossing

Winter St

Washington St

West St

Franklin St

Summer St · Arch St · Otis St

Milk St

Devonshire St

Federal St

FINANCIAL DISTRICT

Congress St

EVELYN MOAKLEY BR.

Tremont St · Mason St

Avery St

Ave. de Lafayette

Chauncy St

Kingston St

High St

Purchase St

Atlantic Ave.

Boylston

Boylston St

Chinatown

Essex St

CHINATOWN

LaGrange

Lincoln St

South St

South Station

0 ——— 0.25 mi
0 ——— 0.25 km

① Boston Common

② Robert Gould Shaw Memorial

③ Massachusetts State House

④ Old Granary Burying Ground

⑤ King's Chapel Burying Ground

⑥ Old City Hall & Benjamin Franklin Statue

⑦ Old State House

⑧ Faneuil Hall

⑨ Faneuil Hall Marketplace

⑩ Boston Harbor Water Shuttle

⑪ Paul Revere House

⑫ Hanover Street

With just 1 day to spend in Boston, focus on the compact downtown area. You'll follow part of the Freedom Trail, which presents an opportunity to explore three-plus centuries of history. My best advice is twofold: Don't concentrate so hard on the trail that you forget to look up and around. And wear comfortable shoes.

START: **Red or Green Line T to Park Street**

1 ★ Boston Common. The oldest public park in the country (bought in 1634, set aside in 1640) is a welcome splash of green in red-brick Boston. As a boy, philosopher Ralph Waldo Emerson herded his mother's cows here on the way to school. ⏱ *5 min. Bordered by Beacon, Park, Tremont, Boylston, and Charles sts. Free admission. Daily 24 hr. T: Red or Green Line to Park Street.*

2 ★★★ Robert Gould Shaw Memorial. The literal and figurative high point of the Common is this magnificent bronze sculpture by Augustus Saint-Gaudens, unveiled in 1897. Read the plaque on the back before or after taking in the incredible artistry of the front, a relief that took 14 years to design and execute. It honors the first American army

Robert Gould Shaw (1837–63) died in battle at Fort Wagner, South Carolina.

unit made up of free black soldiers, the Union Army's 54th Massachusetts Colored Regiment, who fought in the Civil War under the command of Col. Robert Gould Shaw. The sculpture is one of the finest public memorials in the country. ⏱ *10 min. Beacon St. at Park St. Free admission. Daily 24 hr. T: Red or Green Line to Park Street.*

3 ★ Massachusetts State House. The state capitol is one of the signature works of the great Federal-era architect Charles Bulfinch. Note the symmetry, a hallmark of Federal style, in details as large as doors and as small as moldings. Tours (guided and self-guided) explore the building. Allow time to poke around the grounds, which are dotted with statues and monuments; my favorite is President Kennedy captured in midstride. ⏱ *10 min. to explore outside; 40 min. with tour. Beacon St. at Park St.* ☎ *617/727-3676. www.sec.state. ma.us/trs. Free admission and tours. Mon–Fri 9am–5pm (tours 10am–3:30pm). T: Red or Green Line to Park Street.*

4 ★★ Old Granary Burying Ground. Established in 1660 yet not even close to being the oldest in Boston, this cemetery is my favorite for its variety of designs and roster of . . . occupants. Consult the map near the entrance for help in locating the graves of, among others, Paul Revere, Samuel Adams, and John Hancock, whose monument is almost as ostentatious as his signature. For more information, see the

"Boston's Colonial Cemeteries" tour on p 96. 🕐 *15 min. Try to visit in the morning, before tour groups clog the walkways. Tremont St. at Bromfield St. Free admission. Daily 9am–5pm (until 3pm in winter). T: Red or Green Line to Park St.*

⑤ ★ King's Chapel Burying Ground. The oldest graveyard in the city dates to 1630, the same year Europeans settled the peninsula. The chapel was completed in 1754. For more information, see the "Boston's Colonial Cemeteries" tour on p 96. *Tremont St. at School St. Daily 8am–5:30pm (until 3pm in winter). T: Green or Blue Line to Government Center.*

⑥ Old City Hall & Benjamin Franklin Statue. The seat of local government from 1865 to 1969, this ornate French Second Empire building now holds offices and a steakhouse. In front is the city's first portrait statue, a likeness of Benjamin Franklin, who was born a block away. *School St. at City Hall Ave. (end of Province St.). T: Blue or Orange Line to State.*

A simple tombstone at Old Granary Burying Ground.

The Declaration of Independence was read from the Old State House balcony in 1776.

⑦ ★ kids Old State House. Like a flower on the floor of a forest of skyscrapers, this fancy little brick building crouches amid towering neighbors. The Old State House has stood here since 1713, when Massachusetts was a British colony and State Street was named King Street. (In the 1630s, when the Puritan settlement was in its infancy, the whipping post and stocks awaited sinners on this site.) During a visit to Boston in 1789, George Washington watched a parade from the balcony. The building served as the state capitol from Revolutionary times until the present State House opened in 1798. Today it houses the city's history museum, a fascinating amalgamation of permanent and temporary displays. The engaging photographs in the permanent collection, which are featured in many rotating exhibits, are worth the price of admission. On the exterior are vestigial traces of British rule—a lion and a unicorn, both royal symbols that predate the

Revolution. ⏱ *40 min. 206 Washington St., at State St. and Court St.* ☎ *617/720-1713, ext. 21. www.bostonhistory.org. Admission $5 adults, $4 seniors, $1 kids 6–18, free for kids under 6. Daily 9am–5pm (until 6pm July–Aug, until 4pm Jan). T: Blue or Orange Line to State.*

8 ★ **kids Faneuil Hall.** Many of the great orators of the past 2-plus centuries inspired audiences to rebellion, reform, and protest here, earning the building the nickname "the cradle of liberty." One of the best-known speakers was the revolutionary firebrand Samuel Adams (yes, like the beer), whose statue stands outside the Congress Street side of the building. Originally erected in 1742, Faneuil Hall was a gift from prominent merchant Peter Faneuil and was expanded by Charles Bulfinch in 1805. National Park Service rangers give brief but interesting talks in the second-floor auditorium that tell the story. Note the address—Dock Square—and the fact that there isn't a dock, or indeed any water, nearby. The seemingly random shapes and patterns etched into the stone at the foot of the Samuel Adams statue show the shoreline at various points in the past, illustrating how landfill has transformed the city over the years. ⏱ *5 min.; 30 min. for tour. Dock Square (Congress and North sts.).* ☎ *617/242-5675. www.nps.gov/bost. Free admission. Daily*

Samuel Adams was a frequent orator at Faneuil Hall.

9am–5pm; talks every 30 min. until 4:30. T: Green or Blue Line to Government Center, or Orange Line to Haymarket.

9 ★★ **kids Faneuil Hall Marketplace.** The five-building complex incorporates shopping, dining, drinking, live entertainment (think juggling), and people-watching. The Quincy Market building holds a huge food court. At lunch, follow the office workers—lines form at places that earn repeat business. ⏱ *30–60 min. Morning is least busy, but afternoons are most entertaining, especially in warm weather. Bordered by State, Congress, and North sts. and Atlantic Ave.* ☎ *617/523-1300. www.faneuilhallmarketplace.com. Mon–Sat 10am–9pm, Sun noon–6pm; many restaurants open earlier and close later. T: Green Line to Government Center, Orange Line to Haymarket or State, or Blue Line to Aquarium or State.*

10 ★★★ **kids Boston Harbor Water Shuttle.** A classic open secret. The $3 round-trip fare for the commuter ferry that connects downtown Boston and the Charlestown Navy Yard might be the best money you spend during your visit. If time is short, consider riding across the Inner Harbor, turning around, and coming right back. There's plenty to look at on either end: Long Wharf adjoins the New England Aquarium, and the Charlestown pier is near a dramatic Korean War memorial and a 5-minute walk

Top Attractions: Practical Matters

A CityPass (☎ 888/330-5008; www.citypass.com) is a booklet of tickets—so you can go straight to the entrance—to the Harvard Museum of Natural History, the Kennedy library, the New England Aquarium, the Museum of Fine Arts, the Museum of Science, and the Prudential Center Skywalk. If you visit all six, the price ($39 for adults, $19.50 for youths 3–11) gives adults a 50% discount. An even better savings can be in time when lines at the attractions are long—especially if you have your heart set on visiting the aquarium. The passes, good for 1 year from the date of purchase, are on sale at participating attractions, from the website, through the Greater Boston Convention & Visitors Bureau (☎ 800/SEE-BOSTON; www. bostonusa.com), and from some hotel concierge desks and travel agents.

from USS *Constitution* (Old Ironsides) and its museum. But the point is the journey, not the destination—find a place on the deck in good weather, and enjoy feeling the wind in your face as the notion of running away to sea stirs in the back of your mind. In inclement weather, this is still a fun excursion, with excellent views from the enclosed cabin in all but the worst conditions, but do bundle up. ⏲ *10 min. each way, but allow 1 hr. total to include wait time and a bit of exploring at either end; steer clear during the morning and evening rush hours, when regular commuters are all business. Long Wharf, 1 block from State St. and Atlantic Ave.*

The architectural style of the Revere house is usually described as Tudor or folk Gothic.

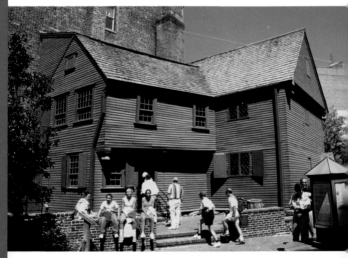

Take a break at a North End cafe to enjoy some cannoli and a cappuccino.

☎ 617/222-4321. www.mbta.com. One-way fare $1.50 adults, 75¢ kids 5–11, free for kids under 5. Mon–Fri 6:30am–8pm, Sat–Sun 10am–6pm. T: Blue Line to Aquarium.

⑪ ★★★ kids Paul Revere House. The more I learn about Paul Revere, the better I understand that he was just a regular guy. On a visit to his North End home, you get a sense of what daily life was like for a successful colonial craftsman. Outfitted with 17th- and 18th-century furniture and fascinating artifacts (including silver pieces created by Revere), the little wood structure is open for self-guided tours, a visitor-friendly format that allows you to set your own pace. A talented silversmith who supported a large family—he had eight children with each of his two wives—Revere played an important role in the fight for independence. As tensions between British troops and colonists escalated in the last years of colonial rule, he monitored the royal soldiers' activities and helped to keep the Americans apprised of the progress of the rebellion. He left this cozy house over and over again, working to bring about what would end up being the American Revolution—and risking his neck every single time. Could I be that brave? Could you? ⏱ *40 min. Crowds fluctuate, but weekend afternoons are busiest. 19 North Sq., between Richmond and Prince sts.* ☎ *617/523-2338. www.paulreverehouse.org. $3 adults, $2.50 seniors and students, $1 kids 5–17, free for kids under 5. Apr–Dec daily 9:30am–5:15pm (until 4:15pm Apr 1–15 & Nov–Dec); Jan–Mar Tues–Sun 9:30am–4:15pm. T: Green or Orange Line to Haymarket.*

⑫ ★★ kids Hanover Street. This crowded street at the heart of the North End, Boston's best-known Italian-American neighborhood, is filled with restaurants, caffès, and out-of-towners. Explore a bit before settling down with a cappuccino, a cannoli, and an appetite for people-watching. My favorites are Mike's Pastry (301 Hanover St., ☎ 617/742-3050, www.mikespastry.com; $) and Caffè Vittoria (296 Hanover St., ☎ 617/227-7606, www.vittoria caffe.com; $). *A tip:* Never call the North End "Little Italy," unless you want everyone around you to know you're a tourist.

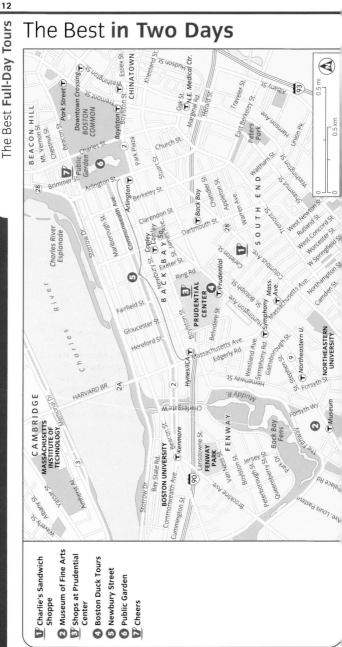

1 Charlie's Sandwich Shoppe
2 Museum of Fine Arts
3 Shops at Prudential Center
4 Boston Duck Tours
5 Newbury Street
6 Public Garden
7 Cheers

If you followed the one-day tour, you have a feel for downtown Boston and its Colonial legacy. In the 19th century, the city spread westward, building up the neighborhood now known as the Back Bay and spreading into the Fenway. Today you'll see a little of everything. Again, comfortable shoes are key. START: **Orange Line T to Back Bay or Green Line T to Copley**

1 ★ kids Charlie's Sandwich Shoppe. The Museum of Fine Arts doesn't open until 10am. Blueberry pancakes at this long-time South End favorite make the time fly by. *429 Columbus Ave. (between Holyoke St. and Braddock Park).* ☎ 617/536-7669. $–$$.

Mary Cassatt's In the Loge.

2 ★★★ kids Museum of Fine Arts. The familiar and the undiscovered meet at the MFA, creating an irresistible atmosphere that makes the museum one of the best in the world. Plan your visit beforehand—you might take a tour, concentrate on a particular period, or head straight to one specific piece. For me, that would probably be a Monet painting (the museum owns dozens), but I reserve the right to substitute a sculpture, a photograph, a mural, a vase, or even a piece of furniture. It's all here; use your time wisely. *See also the mini-tour of the MFA on p. 27.* ⏱ *at least 3 hr. Arrive when the doors open, visit on a weekday if possible, and if you're traveling without kids, try to avoid school vacation weeks. 465 Huntington Ave. (between Museum Rd. and Forsyth Way).* ☎ *617/267-9300. www.mfa. org. Admission (good for 2 visits within 10 days) $15 adults, $13 seniors and students when entire museum is open ($13 and $11 when only West Wing is open), $6.50 kids under 18 on school days before 3pm, otherwise free. Voluntary contribution Wed 4–9:45pm. Entire museum Sat–Tues 10am–4:45pm, Wed 10am–9:45pm, Thurs–Fri 10am–5pm; West Wing only Thurs–Fri 5–9:45pm. Tours Mon–Fri except Mon holidays 10:30am–3pm, Wed 6:15pm, Sat–Sun 11am–3pm. T: Green Line E to Museum or Orange Line to Ruggles.*

3 kids Shops at Prudential Center. The Pru has a good, if generic, food court and several sit-down restaurants (including a branch of Legal Sea Foods; see p 109) that don't require reservations. If the weather's good, picnic in the courtyard. Depending on when your Duck Tour begins (see the next stop), you may want to grab a bite afterward instead. *800 Boylston St.; enter from Huntington Ave. near Belvidere Rd. or from Boylston St. between Fairfield and Gloucester sts.* ☎ *800/SHOP-PRU. www.prudentialcenter.com. $–$$.*

Boston Duck Tour vehicles are comfortable on land and water.

④ ★★★ kids **Boston Duck Tours.** Enjoy the best motorized tour of Boston from a vantage point high above the street in a reconditioned World War II amphibious vehicle. The con-duck-tors (ouch) are exceptionally well trained—they have to be licensed to operate the mammoth "Ducks" on water as well as on land, after which memorizing some historical highlights must feel like child's play. They narrate a relatively brief but thorough tour on land, and then the vehicle rolls down a ramp and cruises around the Charles River basin. Whee! A captivating combination of unusual perspectives, cooling breezes, and fascinating narration. 🕐 *80 min. for tour. Timed tickets go on sale 5 days ahead in person and online; aim for the afternoon, when the action on*

Public Garden, the first botanical garden in the country, is lovely all year-round.

the river is liveliest, but don't pass up a morning tour if that's the only option. Boarding behind the Prudential Center, on Huntington Ave. near Belvidere St., or at the Museum of Science, Science Park, off McGrath–O'Brien Highway (Route 28). ☎ 800/226-7442 or ☎ 617/267-DUCK. www.bostonducktours.com. Tickets $26 adults, $23 seniors and students, $17 kids 3–11, $3 kids under 3. Apr–Nov daily 9am to 30 min. before sunset. No tours Dec–Mar. T: Green Line E to Prudential or any car to Copley for Prudential Center; Green Line to Science Park for Museum of Science.

⑤ ★★★ Newbury Street. The best-known retail destination in New England has something for everyone. Newbury Street is famous for art galleries and designer boutiques, where you can see people glancing at four- and five-figure price tags and not batting an eye. That's mostly at the fancy end—as a rule, the closer to the Public Garden, the nicer the neighborhood. Less expensive and more fun are the stores at higher-numbered addresses. Note that the cross streets go in alphabetical order. *Arlington St. to Massachusetts Ave.* ☎ *617/267-2224. www.newburystreetleague.org. T: Green Line to Arlington, Green Line to* Copley, or Green Line B, C, or D to Hynes/ICA.

⑥ ★★★ kids Public Garden. Boston's most beloved park is a perfect place to unwind. The Public Garden overflows with seasonal blooms and permanent plantings (the roses, which peak in June, are particularly lovely). No matter how crowded it gets, it feels serene. Stroll the perimeter, studying the delightfully miscellaneous collection of monuments and statues. Watch the ducks and the swans. The Swan Boats, which ply the lagoon in the summer, are a lovely reminder of a long-ago, less frantic time. For more information, see the tour of the Public Garden starting on p 90. *Bordered by Arlington, Boylston, Charles, and Beacon sts. Free admission. Daily dawn–dusk. T: Green Line to Arlington.*

⑦ kids Cheers. This is it, in all its touristy glory. I wouldn't even mention it, but it's across the street from the Public Garden, and hardly a week goes by without an out-of-towner asking me for directions. *84 Beacon St. (at Brimmer St.).* ☎ *617/227-9605. www.cheersboston.com. $–$$.*

This flag marks the location of America's most famous bar.

The Best **in Three Days**

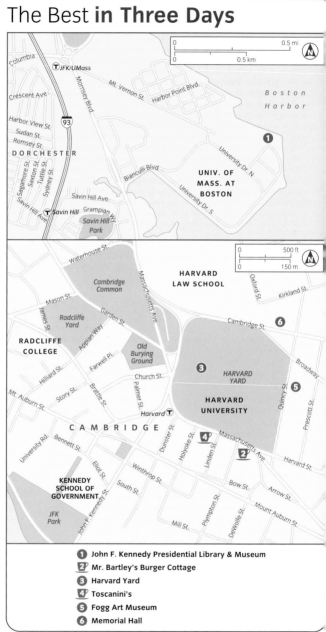

1 John F. Kennedy Presidential Library & Museum

2 Mr. Bartley's Burger Cottage

3 Harvard Yard

4 Toscanini's

5 Fogg Art Museum

6 Memorial Hall

After 2 days concentrating on central Boston, this is your chance to spread out a little. The city's Dorchester neighborhood is accessible on the Red Line and home to a unique attraction, John F. Kennedy's presidential library. His alma mater is just a subway ride away, at the heart of an intriguing city that thrives in Boston's shadow. START: **Red Line to JFK/UMass**

1 ★★★ kids **John F. Kennedy Presidential Library and Museum.** Whether or not you remember the Kennedy era, you'll enjoy this museum. Copious collections of memorabilia, photos, and audio and video recordings illustrate the exhibits, which capture the 35th president in vibrant style. The displays begin with the 1960 presidential campaign; a 17-minute film about his early life narrated by Kennedy himself, using cleverly edited audio clips, kicks off your visit. By the time you reach the dim room where news reports of the assassination play, you'll want to shed a tear along with Walter Cronkite. 🕐 *2 hr. Arrive when the doors open and you may have the place to yourself; prepare for gridlock on summer weekend afternoons. Columbia Point, off University Dr. N. near UMass-Boston.* ☎ *866/ JFK-1960 or* ☎ *617/514-1600. www. jfklibrary.org. Admission $10 adults; $8 seniors, students with ID, and youths 13–17; free for kids under 13.*

Surcharges may apply for special exhibitions. Daily 9am–5pm (last film at 3:55pm). T: Red Line to JFK/UMass, then take free shuttle bus.

2 ★★★ kids **Mr. Bartley's Burger Cottage.** Fantastic burgers are the thing here, but I've also had excellent veggie burgers, hummus, and cheese steaks. Make sure you try the unbelievable onion rings. *1246 Massachusetts Ave. (at Plympton St.), Cambridge.* ☎ *617/354- 6559. $.*

3 ★ **Harvard Yard.** Harvard, the oldest college in the country (founded in 1636), welcomes visitors and offers free guided tours when school is in session. Even without a guide, the stately main campus (two adjoining quads known as Harvard Yard), is worth a look. The most popular stop is the John Harvard statue in front of University Hall. The most popular stop should (according

I. M. Pei designed the Kennedy library to suit its location on Dorchester Bay.

You can always tell a Harvard man, but you can't tell him much.

to me) be Sever Hall, where the rounded archway around the front door forms a "whispering gallery." Stand on one side and speak softly into the molding; someone standing next to you won't be able to hear, but a listener at the other end of the archway will. Sever Hall is next to Memorial Church, which is open to the public except during services. Across the way is majestic Widener Library; climb the steps for a sensational view of this part of the campus. To begin exploring, visit the website or stop in at the Events & Information Center to take a tour or pick up a map. ⏲ *30 min.; longer if you take a tour. Events & Information Center, 1350 Massachusetts Ave. (between Dunster and Holyoke sts.)* ☎ *617/495-1573. www.harvard.edu. Tours Mon–Sat; check website for schedule. T: Red Line to Harvard.*

---

4 ★★★ **kids Toscanini's.** A break already? Hey, college is hard! You *need* gourmet ice cream, in flavors both plain and fancy. Join the real college students and take your treat across the street, then find somewhere to perch in the Yard. *1310 Massachusetts Ave. (between Holyoke and Linden sts.).* ☎ *617/354-9350. $.*

5 ★★ **Fogg Art Museum.** The Fogg is not too small and not too big; it's just right. The collections are both classic and contemporary, without an overwhelming emphasis on anything. I particularly like the 19th-century American and European paintings and drawings, but I'm easily distracted by everything from contemporary sculpture to Flemish landscape painting. The Fogg adjoins the Busch-Reisinger Museum, which specializes in art of northern and central Europe, and is a block away from the Arthur M. Sackler Museum, the university's repository of Asian and ancient art. I have a soft spot for the Fogg, but you may prefer one of the others. One admission fee covers all three—explore away. ⏲ *2 hr. Seldom truly mobbed, except during special exhibitions or when a large class is studying a particular work (which can be fun if the students know their stuff). 32 Quincy St. (at Broadway).* ☎ *617/495-9400. www.artmuseums.harvard.edu. Admission to Fogg, Busch-Reisinger, and Sackler museums $7.50 adults, $6 seniors and students, free for kids under 18; free for everyone before noon Sat. Mon–Sat 10am–5pm; Sun 1–5pm. T: Red Line to Harvard.*

6 ★ **Memorial Hall.** Anything but a stereotypical red-brick Harvard building, "Mem Hall" is a Victorian-era (1874) structure in an unusual style known as Ruskin Gothic. Polychrome (multicolored) brickwork sets off quirky archways, and the floor plan mimics a Gothic cathedral, with a dining hall in place of the nave and Sanders Theatre, a lecture and concert hall, in the apse. The transept is a hall of memorials that lists the Harvard men who perished in the Civil War, but only if they fought for the Union. ⏲ *10 min. Stay away during mealtimes to avoid being trampled by hungry students. 45 Quincy St. (at Cambridge St.).* ●

Boston with Kids

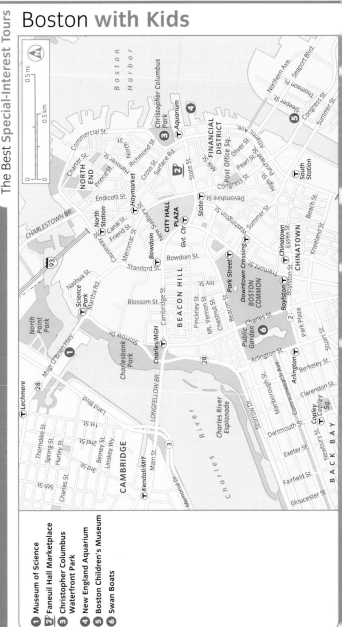

1 Museum of Science
2 Faneuil Hall Marketplace
3 Christopher Columbus Waterfront Park
4 New England Aquarium
5 Boston Children's Museum
6 Swan Boats

Every day in the summer, children shuffle along the Freedom Trail like prisoners on a chain gang, looking hot, bored, and tired. Unless your kids are old enough to express an interest, spare them. Boston offers so much else to see and do that you'll never miss the Freedom Trail. Before you plunge in, note that I suggest you visit either stop 4 or stop 5 (not both) depending on how old your kids are. START: **Green Line T to Science Park**

① ★★★
Museum of Science. This is the best indoor family destination in the Boston area. It can be a bit overwhelming, with some 500 exhibits— engaging hands-on activities and experiments, interactive displays, and fascinating demonstrations—but it's both educational and entertaining. I suggest that you pick a few subjects you find interesting and build your visit around them. For example, I especially like the sections that

A Tyrannosaur at the Museum of Science.

focus on the human body, dinosaurs, and the science of light (including a small lighthouse). Use their website before you leave home to rough out a route through the enormous museum, leaving room for inspiration to strike; the temporary exhibits are always worth a look. Also check the schedules for the Omni theater, planetarium, and laser shows, which can help you decide whether to budget the time and money for a longer stay—or a return visit. ⏱ *3 hr. Buy tickets online in advance and arrive at 9am sharp to avoid the largest crowds. Science Park, off O'Brien Hwy. (Rte. 28).* ☎ *617/723-2500. www. mos.org. Museum admission $15 adults, $13 seniors, $13 kids 3–11, free for kids under 3. Omni theater, planetarium, or laser show $9 adults, $8 seniors, $7 kids.*

Learn about electricity at a dramatic demonstration of the Van de Graaf generator at the Museum of Science.

Discounted combination tickets available. Sat–Thurs 9am–5pm (until 7pm July 5 to Labor Day), Fri 9am–9pm; theaters close later. T: Green Line to Science Park.

2 ★★ Faneuil Hall Marketplace.
The counters that line both sides of Quincy Market are a smorgasbord with something for everyone, from the hungriest omnivore to the pickiest vegetarian. Get your food to go, because you'll be picnicking across the street, away from the largest crowds. See p 9, bullet 9.

3 ★★ Christopher Columbus Waterfront Park.
Hidden in plain sight a stone's throw from Faneuil Hall Marketplace is this lovely little park overlooking a marina. It has a small playground (to your left as you face the water), plenty of lawns and shady trees, a rose garden, benches beneath the enormous trellis, and an excellent fountain. The fountain doesn't run all the time; you have to press a button (there are four) arranged around the edge to start the timed spray. ⏱ *45 min. Atlantic Ave. (State and Richmond sts.).* ☎ *617/635-4505. www.ci.boston. ma.us/parks. T: Blue Line to Aquarium.*

4 ★ New England Aquarium.
Consider skipping this stop or the next one, depending on how old your kids are and whether marine life interests them. For preteens and teens who like aquariums, the thousands of fish and aquatic mammals here make this place a big hit. The centerpiece is the Giant Ocean Tank, where the sharks are. The surrounding displays and hands-on exhibits are home to a vast variety of sea creatures. My favorites are the penguins (I especially like the little blues, which are native to Australia) and the medical center, a working veterinary hospital that treats patients from all over the region, including stranded, injured, and rescued animals. Other exhibits focus on jellyfish, the Amazon, the Gulf of Maine, and tide pools. Allow an extra hour if you plan to take in a 3D film in the adjacent theater. ⏱ *2 hr. Invest in a Boston CityPass (see p 10) to avoid the lines at the entrance. Central Wharf (½ block from State St. and Atlantic Ave.).* ☎ *617/973-5200. www.newengland aquarium.org. Admission $18 adults, $10 kids 3–11, free for kids under 3. Imax theater tickets $9.50 adults, $7.50 kids. Aquarium July to Labor Day Mon–Thurs 9am–6pm, Fri–Sun & holidays 9am–7pm; day after Labor Day to June Mon–Fri 9am–5pm,*

View seals, penguins, sharks, crabs, and fish galore at the New England Aquarium.

Kids climbing the walls? Take them to the Boston Children's Museum to burn off some energy.

Sat–Sun 9am–6pm. Imax theater daily 9:30am–10:30pm. T: Blue Line to Aquarium.

⑤ ★★ Boston Children's Museum. If your kids are under 11 or so, or don't care for fish and their friends, skip the aquarium and head here. This is hands-on heaven: Kids can dress up in costumes, pilot a boat, shop in a supermarket, visit Japan, learn about Boston's black community, make giant soap bubbles, and climb around in a gigantic two-story maze. And that's just scratching the surface. ⏱ *2 hr. Crowds are especially large on rainy summer weekdays. 300 Congress St. (Sleeper St., overlooking Fort Point Channel).* ☎ *617/426-8855. www.bostonkids.org. Admission $9 adults, $7 seniors and kids 2–15, free for kids under 2; $1 for everyone Fri after 5pm. Sat–Thurs 10am–5pm, Fri 10am–9pm. T: Red Line to South Station, 10-min. walk.*

⑥ ★★ Swan Boats. End a day of interactive experiences and running around with something low-tech and sedentary: a ride on a Swan Boat. Pedaling one of these things looks like brutally hard work—for the attendants at the back of each boat who actually do the pedaling. Meanwhile, the passengers relax on long benches, taking in the passing scene of ducks, swans, pigeons, dogs, and humans lazing around the beautiful Public Garden. The swan-drawn boat in the opera *Lohengrin* inspired the design of the vessels, which have been operated by the Paget family since 1877; the current fleet consists of larger versions of the originals. If you're a fiend for planning, make sure your family is familiar with E. B. White's charming novel *The Trumpet of the Swan* before you even see a Swan Boat—you won't be sorry. ⏱ *15 min. for the ride; allow 1 hr., including a little down time before or after. The Public Garden is bordered by Arlington, Boylston, Charles, and Beacon sts.; the boats operate on the lagoon in the middle.* ☎ *617/522-1966. www.swanboats.com. Tickets $2.50 adults, $2 seniors, $1 kids 2–15. Mid-Apr to mid-June daily 10am–4pm; mid-June to Labor Day daily 10am–5pm; day after Labor Day to mid-Sept Mon–Fri noon–4pm, Sat–Sun 10am–4pm. Closed mid-Sept to mid-Apr. T: Green Line to Arlington.*

The Fenway

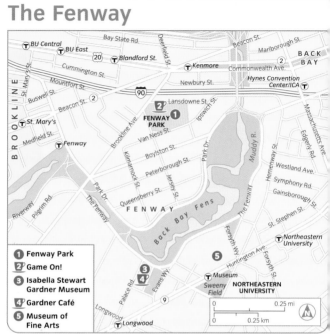

1. Fenway Park
2. Game On!
3. Isabella Stewart Gardner Museum
4. Gardner Café
5. Museum of Fine Arts

The Fenway neighborhood offers a unique opportunity to visit two institutions that are virtual temples in their fields: Fenway Park and the Museum of Fine Arts. Weird combination? Maybe a little. But consider this: Both places celebrate the efforts of people who do what they do better than just about anyone else. START: **Green Line T (B, C, or D train) to Kenmore**

1 ★★★ kids Fenway Park. The oldest and arguably most beloved venue in the major leagues is Fenway, which John Updike famously described as a "lyric little bandbox of a ball park." Cubs and Yankees fans are likeliest to argue, but even they can't deny the appeal of Fenway, which opened in 1912. The magic isn't in the players or the games or the unforgettable green of the playing field or even the story of the supposed "curse" that prevailed in the 86 years between World Series titles (1918–2004). It's in the whole experience, and you can't truly understand what all the fuss is about until you see for yourself. You don't have to score scarce, expensive tickets to do so, either—tours run year-round. Tour specifics may vary, especially in the off-season, when construction is usually going on. Visitors usually get to explore the stands and visit the press box and luxury seats, and they sometimes walk on the warning track and touch the left-field wall, nicknamed the "Green Monster." ⏱ 1½ hr. 4 **Yawkey Way (Brookline Ave.). Tours**

museum makes a perfect stop between Fenway Park and the Museum of Fine Arts; its namesake was a devoted Red Sox fan. An heiress and socialite, "Mrs. Jack" Gardner (1840–1924) was also an avid traveler and patron of the arts. The core of the museum, which opened in 1903, is her private collection of paintings, sculpture, furniture, tapestries, and decorative objects. It includes works by Titian, Botticelli, Raphael, Rembrandt, Matisse, and Sargent. My favorite gallery is the Dutch Room, where the displays include a 17th-century German sculpture of an ostrich made out of silver and an actual ostrich egg. The largest artifact is the building itself, constructed from 1899 to 1901 and designed to resemble a 15th-century Venetian palace. Three floors of galleries surround the plant- and flower-filled courtyard. Although the terms of Mrs. Gardner's will forbid changing the permanent exhibitions, the museum is a lively presence in the contemporary art world, sponsoring artists in residence and making long-term expansion plans.

🕐 *2 hr. 280 The Fenway (Museum Rd.).* ☎ *617/566-1401. www.gardnermuseum.org. Admission adults $11 weekends, $10 weekdays; $7*

Fenway's "Green Monster."

meet at the Souvenir Store, 19 Yawkey Way. ☎ *617/226-6666 for tour info;* ☎ *877/733-7699 for game tickets. www.redsox.com. Tours $12 adults, $11 seniors, $10 kids 2–15, free for kids under 2. Daily 9am–4pm or until 3 hr. before game time. T: Green Line B, C, or D to Kenmore or D to Fenway.*

2 **kids Game On!** The chow here is several crucial notches better than ballpark food—though you can get an excellent dog or burger. *82 Lansdowne St. (Brookline Ave.).* ☎ *617/351-7001. $–$$.*

3 ★★ **Isabella Stewart Gardner Museum.** This engaging

The Gardner museum courtyard.

John Singer Sargent's famous portrait of Isabella Stewart Gardner.

adults named Isabella with ID. Tues–Sun (and some Mon holidays) 11am–5pm. T: Green Line E to Museum.

4 ★★ **Gardner Café.** The Gardner Museum has an appropriately classy cafe that's a perfect place to indulge in some sweets and a cup of tea or a glass of wine. *280 The Fenway (Museum Rd.).* ☎ *617/566-1401.* $–$$.

5 ★★★ kids **Museum of Fine Arts.** The MFA is more than just art; its architecture is noteworthy, too. Today, an enormous expansion is in the early stages. The British architect Sir Norman Foster designed the project, which will enclose a courtyard and add some 151,000 square feet (14,028sq. m) of space. The work may require the closure of some galleries, so I'll spotlight something that isn't going anywhere—the rotunda. See p 13, bullet **2**.

seniors; $5 college students with ID; free for kids under 18 and

Cyrus Dallini's Appeal to the Great Spirit, outside the Museum of Fine Arts.

Museum of Fine Arts

Gund Gallery

5B

5C

Loring Gallery

Antioch Mosaic

Rabb Gallery

Floor 2

Foster Gallery

West Wing/ Museum Road Entrance

Calderwood Courtyard

Garden Court

Torf Gallery

Trustman Galleries

Huntington Entrance

Floor 1

5A

Most visitors enter the Museum of Fine Arts through I. M. Pei's West Wing (1981), but the Huntington Avenue entrance to the original (1909) building is far more interesting. It overlooks a lawn where you'll find **5A** *Appeal to the Great Spirit*, a bronze statue of an Indian on horseback. Cast in Paris in 1909, it's one of the finest works by American sculptor Cyrus Dallin.

Inside, a sweeping staircase leads to the rotunda, which holds one of the museum's signature elements: **5B** **John Singer Sargent's Rotunda Murals.** Sargent incorporated sculpture and architectural features with paintings to create the elaborate space; colorful murals depict mythological figures such as Apollo, Athena, the Muses, and Prometheus.

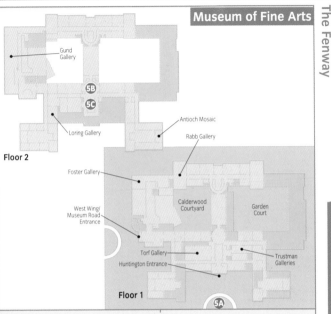

The rotunda, which opened to the public in 1921, proved so popular that the museum wanted more. Return to the staircase, scoot out of the flow of traffic, and look up and around to take in Sargent's **5C** **Colonnade Murals.** Creating this space required substantial structural work; for example, the columns that allow light to pour in replaced solid walls. Apollo is here, too, as is a delightfully grisly representation of Perseus holding Medusa's severed head. This project was Sargent's final work: In 1925, the night before he was to sail from London to Boston to supervise installation of the last section, he died in his sleep.

Detail of Renoir's Dance at Bougival.

Copley Square Architecture

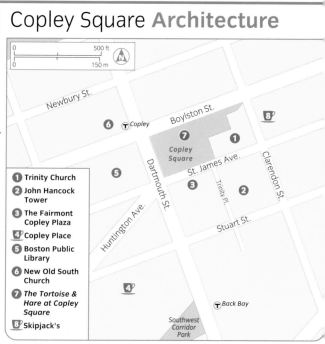

1 **Trinity Church**

2 **John Hancock Tower**

3 **The Fairmont Copley Plaza**

4 **Copley Place**

5 **Boston Public Library**

6 **New Old South Church**

7 **The Tortoise & Hare at Copley Square**

8 **Skipjack's**

Copley Square is an architectural treasure. Landmark build-ings occupy three sides of the lovely plaza, notable structures peek in from two corners, and a constant flow of pedestrians enlivens the area. The square is most enjoyable on Tuesday and Fri-day afternoons from July to November, when a farmers' market anchors one side, but it's a visual treat year-round. START: **Green Line T to Copley**

1 ★★★ **Trinity Church.** One of the best-known church buildings in the country, Trinity Church is archi-tect H. H. Richardson's masterwork. A native of New Orleans and a Har-vard graduate, Richardson was a larger-than-life figure whose style was so distinctive that it now bears his name: Richardsonian Romanesque. Think of the prototypi-cal New England church: white with a towering steeple. Trinity is any-thing but. Before you enter, stand

across the square and take a moment to enjoy the busy yet har-monious design of the polychrome (multicolored) exterior. Consecrated in 1877, the building is granite, trimmed with red sandstone, with a roof of red tiles on the 221-foot (67m) tower. Inside, barrel vaults draw the eye up to the 63-foot (19m) ceilings, and John La Farge's murals and decorative painting make imaginative use of colored plaster that complements the hues

Trinity Church.

in the renowned stained-glass windows. Be sure to spend some time contemplating La Farge's window *Christ in Majesty,* in the west gallery. And take a tour, which will surely touch on the building's remarkable construction—the structure rests on 4,502 pilings driven into the mud that was once the Back Bay; the pilings must be kept wet so they don't rot. ⏱ *1 hr. 206 Clarendon St. (Boylston St.).* ☎ *617/536-0944. www.trinitychurchboston.org. Free admission. Tour $5. Daily 8am–6pm. T: Green Line to Copley.*

② ★★ John Hancock Tower. This reflecting-glass behemoth is remarkable for what it isn't—obtrusive, distracting, or incongruous. It complements rather than competes with its neighbors, and it's so beautiful that I can almost forgive the wind-tunnel effect it creates for several blocks in all directions. While still under construction, the Hancock Tower gained worldwide notoriety for some unfortunate incidents in which huge panes of glass plummeted onto the sidewalk hundreds of feet below. (Yes, it was over 30 years ago, and the problem was corrected quickly, but it's still a great story.) The top-floor observation deck, for many years one of the most popular attractions in

Boston, closed in 2001. *200 Clarendon St. (St. James Ave.)*

③ ★ The Fairmont Copley Plaza. The relatively austere facade of the 1912 hotel conceals a riotously ornate interior that's well worth a look. (Bonus: A black Labrador named Catie Copley hangs around in the lobby, and you can probably pet her if she's there.) Architect Henry Janeway Hardenbergh also designed New York's Plaza Hotel. *138 St. James Ave.*

④ Copley Place. Boston's fanciest shopping center has a limited selection of places to grab a quick bite, but it's a good climate-controlled option for resting and refueling. *100 Huntington Ave.* ☎ *617/236-5800. $.*

⑤ ★★ Boston Public Library. Architect Charles Follen McKim of the legendary New York firm of McKim, Mead & White gets the credit for designing the main branch of the city's library system, but he was really the captain of an artistic

The 60-story Hancock tower is the tallest building in New England.

The Boston Public Library opened in 1895.

all-star team. Take a tour if it fits into your schedule, or explore on your own. Pause outside to admire the way the arches across the granite facade of the Renaissance Revival building echo the design of Trinity Church, on the other side of the square. The library's bronze doors are the work of sculptor Daniel Chester French (better known for the seated Abraham Lincoln at the presidential memorial in Washington, D.C., and the John Harvard Statue in Cambridge), and Augustus Saint-Gaudens created the decorative seals above each of the three entrance arches. Inside, sculpture, painting, and elaborate architectural details abound. The walls of the entrance hall are rare yellow Siena marble, and the murals on the staircase and in the second-floor corridor, which represent the wisdom and knowledge collected in the building, are by Pierre Puvis de Chavannes. On the third floor is the Sargent Gallery, which houses John Singer Sargent's murals illustrating religious themes. The celebrated portraitist worked on the murals from 1895 through 1916, and no matter how many times you view them, you'll always notice something new. Many consider this gallery their favorite part of the library, but I love the interior courtyard, with its Roman arcade and eternally peaceful atmosphere. ⏱ *1 hr. 700 Boylston St. (Dartmouth St.).*

☎ *617/536-5400. www.bpl.org. Mon–Thurs 9am–9pm, Fri–Sat 9am–5pm, Sun (Oct–May only) 1–5pm. Art & Architecture Tours free. Tours Mon 2:30pm, Tues & Thurs 6pm, Fri–Sat 11am, Sun (Oct–May only) 2pm. T: Green Line to Copley.*

⑥ ★ New Old South Church.
The Northern Italian Gothic church anchors its corner of Copley Square with authority. The multicolored facade (the technical term for the design on the entrance arches is zebra-striped) encloses a similarly vivid sanctuary, illuminated with stained glass throughout. Be sure to visit the chapel, to the left as you enter, where the Gothic influence is particularly evident in the design of the windows. Wondering about the name? The congregation of this church, constructed from 1872 through 1875, originated downtown in the building now known as the Old South Meeting House. *645 Boylston St.* ☎ *617/536-1970. www. oldsouth.org. Mon–Fri 9am–7pm, Sat 10am–4pm, Sun 9am–4pm. T: Green Line to Copley.*

⑦ ★ kids The Tortoise & Hare at Copley Square. Trinity Church
and the library are Copley Square's best-known features, but this neighborhood is equally famous for being home to the finish line of the Boston Marathon—which is painted on the street outside the Boylston Street

entrance to the library and stays there year-round. In the middle of Copley Square is a whimsical reminder of the annual athletic event, a three-dimensional illustration of the tortoise and hare fable created by Nancy Schön (also the sculptor of *Make Way for Ducklings,* in the Public Garden). *Off Boylston St. between Clarendon and Dartmouth sts.*

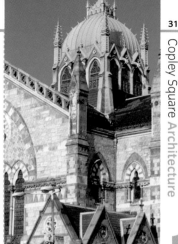

New Old South Church.

8 ★ kids Skipjack's. This fancy-looking seafood restaurant, which serves all afternoon, has a welcoming bar for adults and a special menu for kids. *199 Clarendon St. (Boylston St. and St. James Ave.)* ☎ *617/536-3500. $–$$$.*

Newbury Street

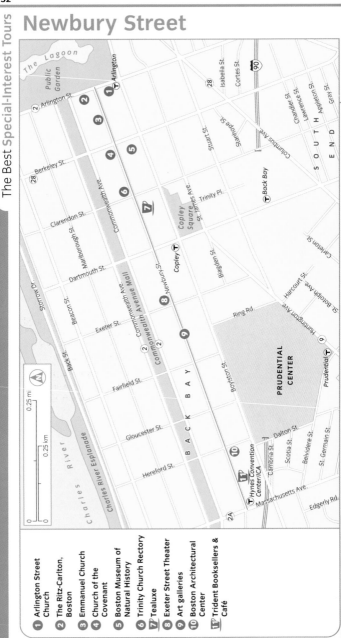

1 Arlington Street Church
2 The Ritz-Carlton, Boston
3 Emmanuel Church
4 Church of the Covenant
5 Boston Museum of Natural History
6 Trinity Church Rectory
7 Tealuxe
8 Exeter Street Theater
9 Art galleries
10 Boston Architectural Center
11 Trident Booksellers & Café

N ewbury Street, Boston's foremost retail destination, is also an architectural landmark. The Back Bay neighborhood, originally a marshy body of water, was created when 19th-century landfill projects replaced the "bay" with dry land. For modern-day visitors, the result is a harmonious blend of sightseeing and shopping. START: **Green Line T to Arlington**

1 ★ Arlington Street Church.
Constructed from 1859 to 1861, this was the first building completed in the Back Bay (the congregation dates to 1729). Architect Arthur Gilman designed the exterior to resemble the Church of St. Martin-in-the-Fields in London's Trafalgar Square. The Italianate interior is famous for the stained-glass windows designed by Louis Comfort Tiffany; they're considered some of the celebrated artist's finest work. Like Trinity Church in Copley Square, this building rests on wooden pilings. ⏲ *30 min. 351 Boylston St. (Arlington St.)* ☎ *617-536-7050. www.ascboston.org. Visit office to be admitted to sanctuary. Mon–Fri 9am–5pm (closed Fri in summer), Sat–Sun 1–5pm. T: Green Line to Arlington.*

2 ★ The Ritz-Carlton, Boston.
The exterior of the Ritz-Carlton, the original hotel in the luxury chain, blends Regency and Art Deco details. It opened in 1927 and was once so exclusive that management

The door pulls on the Lesley Lindsey Memorial Chapel.

evaluated prospective guests based on whether their names appeared in the Social Register or *Who's Who. 15 Arlington St. (Newbury St.)*

3 Emmanuel Church. The main part of the church was the first building completed on Newbury Street, in 1862. The Gothic Revival exterior unites three separate spaces; the loveliest is the Leslie Lindsey Memorial Chapel, which was consecrated in 1924. It bears the name of a Bostonian who died on her honeymoon in 1915 when a German U-boat torpedoed the *Lusitania.* Look closely at the stained-glass window representing St. Cecilia, which was modeled on the young bride. She died wearing the diamonds and rubies her father had given her as a wedding gift; her parents sold the jewels to finance the construction of the chapel. ⏲ *30 min. 15 Newbury St. (Arlington St.).* ☎ *617-536-3355. www.emmanuel-boston.org. T: Green Line to Arlington.*

The oldest continuously operating Ritz-Carlton hotel in the United States.

④ ★ Church of the Covenant. The Church of the Covenant is an interesting complement to Emmanuel Church; both were constructed in Gothic Revival style. Erected from 1865 to 1867, the church has an elaborately decorated 240-foot (73m) steeple, which Oliver Wendell Holmes described as "absolutely perfect." (Emmanuel doesn't have a steeple.) Louis Comfort Tiffany and John La Farge designed the stained-glass windows, which were created by three of Tiffany's most esteemed artists. The best known is the Sparrow Window, which depicts Jesus at work, but I prefer St. Augustine, who sits beneath a passage of his own writing incorporated into the design (like graffiti!). The parish house holds Gallery NAGA (p 79), which specializes in contemporary art. ⏱ *30 min. 67 Newbury St. (Berkeley St.).* ☎ *617/266-7480. www.church ofthecovenant.org. Daily hours. T: Green Line to Arlington.*

⑤ Boston Museum of Natural History. The 1864 building, a graceful French Academic design by

Church of the Covenant's steeple.

William Preston, now houses the prestigious fashion retailer Louis Boston. The museum—a forerunner of the Museum of Science—is long gone; originally a two-story structure, it retained its original roof when the building gained a third floor. *234 Berkeley St. (Newbury and Boylston sts.)*

⑥ Trinity Church Rectory. H. H. Richardson designed the rectory, which was completed in 1879, 2 years after the church (p 28, bullet ①). The style is considered Richardsonian Romanesque, but this building is considerably less elaborate than the landmark house of worship. *233 Clarendon St. (Newbury St.)*

⑦ ★ Tealuxe. An encyclopedic selection of teas (all of the chai selections are great) complements sweets and snacks upstairs, downstairs, and out on the patio. *108 Newbury St.* ☎ *617/927-0400. $.*

⑧ Exeter Street Theater. The 1884 Romanesque Revival building (get a load of the top-floor ornamentation on both the Exeter St. and Newbury St. sides) originally housed the First Spiritualist Temple. It was later a movie theater and now holds office space. *26 Exeter St. (Newbury St. and Commonwealth Ave.)*

⑨ ★★ Art galleries. Not all of the art on Newbury Street is bricks and mortar (or granite or pudding-stone or other building materials)— the tony thoroughfare is far better known for its huge concentration of art galleries. Take time now to check out some painting, sculpture, photography, or other work. Turn to the "Art" section of chapter 4 for specific suggestions. A good strategy if you're not heading straight to a particular destination is to pick up a copy of the free *Gallery Guide*

Tired of gallery-hopping? Take a load off at one of Newbury Street's many outdoor cafes.

magazine, available at many Newbury Street businesses, and target a couple of appealing shows. Alternatively, as you walk along, pick up places to which you'd like to return. Be sure to keep an eye out for galleries below and above street level.

⑩ ★ Boston Architectural Center. Although the BAC is an example of Brutalist architecture, the large glass windows on the Hereford Street side make it far more appealing than another notable local Brutalist building, the inexcusable Boston City Hall. Take a couple of minutes to walk around to the Boylston Street side of the BAC to see my favorite element: a whimsical trompe l'oeil mural of a classical building by Richard Haas. The firm of Ashley, Meyer & Associates won a national competition to design this building, which opened in 1966. Founded in 1889, the BAC is a lively institution that offers bachelor's degrees, master's degrees, and continuing-ed programs. It exhibits work of interest to the design community (not just student and faculty shows) in two public spaces: the McCormick Gallery, in the lobby, and the fourth-floor Stankowicz Gallery. *320 Newbury St. (Hereford St.).* ☎ *617/262-5000. www.the-bac.edu. Galleries Mon–Thurs 8:30am–10:30pm, Fri 8:30am–9pm, Sat 9am–5pm, Sun noon–7pm. T: Green Line B, C, or D to Hynes/ICA.*

⑪ ★★ Trident Booksellers & Cafe. This is the perfect place to wind down—it offers good food, drink, books, and people-watching. *338 Newbury St.* ☎ *617/267-8688. $.*

Hidden Cambridge

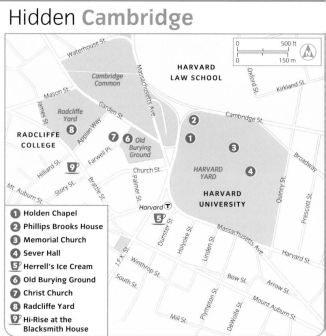

HARVARD
LAW SCHOOL

Cambridge
Common

Radcliffe
Yard

RADCLIFFE
COLLEGE

Old
Burying
Ground

HARVARD
YARD

HARVARD
UNIVERSITY

Harvard Ⓣ

1 **Holden Chapel**
2 **Phillips Brooks House**
3 **Memorial Church**
4 **Sever Hall**
5 **Herrell's Ice Cream**
6 **Old Burying Ground**
7 **Christ Church**
8 **Radcliffe Yard**
9 **Hi-Rise at the Blacksmith House**

The beaten track in and around Harvard Square is beaten indeed—for example, eager photographers wore down the lawn across from the John Harvard Statue in Harvard Yard so thoroughly that the university finally paved over the bare earth of the shutterbugs' favorite spot. But even this frenzied neighborhood offers some pockets of peace and (relative) quiet. START: **Red Line to Harvard**

① ★ **Holden Chapel.** Between the main part of busy Harvard Yard and busy Massachusetts Avenue (on the other side of the wall) is a tiny Georgian building with an interesting history. Completed in 1744, it was a chapel only for about the first 20 years of its existence. It was also a garage, a storeroom, office space, barracks for Revolutionary War troops serving under George Washington, and an anatomy lab. Today it's a classroom and a rehearsal space for undergraduate choral groups. *Harvard Yard, off Massachusetts Ave. near Peabody and Cambridge sts.*

② ★ **Phillips Brooks House.** The quietest corner of the Yard is home to Phillips Brooks House (1899), the name of both the building and the public-service association that makes its headquarters here. *Harvard Yard, off Cambridge St.*

③ ★★ **Memorial Church.** The university's church was dedicated in 1932 in memory of those who had died in what was then optimistically called the Great War. Sculptures and plaques commemorate the dead; the south wall, to the right as you enter, lists their names. (They include Joseph P. Kennedy, Jr., the president's brother, class of 1938.) Nondenominational Protestant services (including morning prayer, Mon–Sat 8:45–9am) are open to the public. ⏱ *30 min.* ☎ *617/495-5508. www.memorialchurch.harvard.edu. Harvard Yard, near Broadway and Cambridge St.*

4 ★★★ **Sever Hall.** H. H. Richardson, the architect of Boston's Trinity Church, designed Sever (rhymes with "believer"), a classroom building that opened in 1880 and drives architects wild. They rave about the brickwork, the chimneys, the roof, and even the window openings. Not being an architect, I love it because if you stand to one side of the front door and whisper into the archway, someone standing next to you can't hear a thing, but someone at the other end of the arch can hear you loud and clear. Try it! *Harvard Yard, off Quincy St.*

5 ★ **Herrell's Ice Cream.** The specialty here is mixing candy, cookies, and other goodies into the ice cream, but I'm a sucker for the incredible hot fudge. *15 Dunster St.* ☎ *617/497-2179. $.*

6 ★★ **Old Burying Ground.** This cemetery, sometimes called the Cambridge Burying Ground, was established in 1635, a year before the founding of the university. Thousands of people rush past every day, and only the tiniest fraction venture inside the fence. They're missing a fascinating experience. As you explore the compact area, some 2 centuries' worth of examples can help you trace evolving fashions in gravestones. ⏱ *30 min. Massachusetts Ave. (Garden St.)*

7 **Christ Church.** This is the oldest standing church building in Cambridge; it opened in 1761, and was designed by Peter Harrison. It's wood, with a square tower and some longstanding war wounds: British muskets made the bullet holes in the vestibule during the Revolution. ⏱ *10 min. Zero Garden St.* ☎ *617/876-0200. www.cccambridge.org.*

8 **Radcliffe Yard.** Founded as the Harvard Annex in 1879 and chartered as Radcliffe College in 1894, Harvard's "sister school" existed—at least on paper—until 1999. The creation of the Radcliffe Institute for Advanced Study completed a process that began in 1943, when Radcliffe students first gained admission to Harvard classrooms. Harvard Yard is large and dramatic, with people racing every which way; Radcliffe Yard is an enclave of serenity. It consists of red-brick buildings executed in typical New England college style (Greek Revival and Federal). *Appian Way (Garden and Brattle sts.)*

9 **Hi-Rise at the Blacksmith House.** Longfellow gave this building its name in the poem about the "spreading chestnut tree." An excellent artisan bread company handles the baking. *56 Brattle St.* ☎ *617/492-3003. $–$$.*

The interior of Christ Church.

Romantic Boston

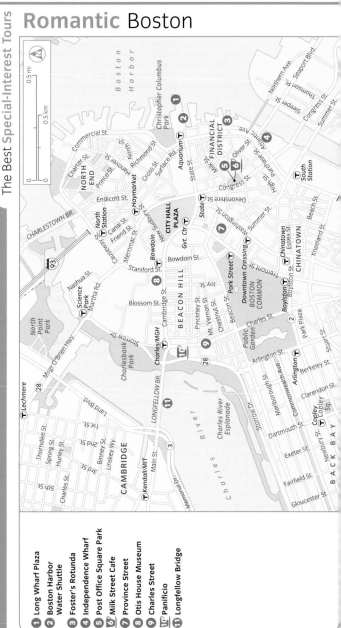

1 Long Wharf Plaza
2 Boston Harbor
   Water Shuttle
3 Foster's Rotunda
4 Independence Wharf
5 Post Office Square Park
6 Milk Street Cafe
7 Province Street
8 Otis House Museum
9 Charles Street
10 Panificio
11 Longfellow Bridge

You and your sweetie are in an unfamiliar city, and I'm sending you on an unfamiliar route, across town from one body of water to another. It's fun no matter when you set out, as long as you get to the Otis House Museum in time for the last tour, at 4:30pm. You're rebels, traveling roughly perpendicular to the Freedom Trail, off the beaten path. It's the two of you against the world. See? Bonding already. START: **Blue Line to Aquarium**

① ★★ **Long Wharf Plaza.** Surrounded by water on three sides, in view of the airport and most of the harbor ferry and sightseeing-boat routes, this little plaza is a perfect front-row seat for a busy seaport. The lovely design on the ground next to the flagpole is a useful decoration known as a compass rose. ⏲ *At least 10 min. Long Wharf (end of State St.).*

② ★★★ **Boston Harbor Water Shuttle.** Some commuter boats go to distant suburbs; the smaller ones are local. Getting out on the water is the best part of the experience of taking a narrated cruise, and riding to Charlestown and back on your own costs far less than a formal tour. If you didn't have time to visit the plaza on Long Wharf before jumping on the water shuttle, allow time when you return. ⏲ *1 hr. See p 9, bullet* ⑩.

③ ★ **Foster's Rotunda.** The ninth-floor balcony provides an awe-inspiring perspective on Boston Harbor, Logan Airport, and the Seaport District. Be prepared to skip this stop in favor of Independence Wharf when there's a private function in the rotunda (the lobby security staff will turn you away) and on weekends. ⏲ *30 min. You may have to show ID, sign in, or both. 30 Rowes Wharf (Atlantic Ave. between High St. and Old Northern Ave.), in the Boston Harbor Hotel complex. Mon–Fri 11am–4pm. T: Blue Line to Aquarium or Red Line to South Station.*

④ ★ **Independence Wharf.** Independence Wharf is more likely to be open when you visit than Foster's Rotunda, but the view isn't as amazing. If you've already been there, you can skip this stop. If not, the 14th-floor vistas of Boston Harbor and the

Long Wharf.

Fort Point Channel from here are worth your time. 🕐 *30 min. You may have to show ID, sign in, or both. 470 Atlantic Ave. (Moakley Bridge at Seaport Blvd.). Daily 11am–5pm. T: Red Line to South Station or Blue Line to Aquarium.*

⑤ ★ Post Office Square Park. This gorgeous park stands on land that once held an ugly municipal garage. A visionary redevelopment project moved the parking into a new underground facility (it's been called the "Garage Mahal") and created an arrangement under which the revenues from below help support the green space above. The beautifully groomed park has free wireless Internet access and a fountain for dogs, with water flowing at their mouth level. The 1.7-acre (.69ha) space, formally Norman B. Leventhal Park, sits at the heart of the Financial District and enjoys the distinction of being one of the busiest warm-weather pickup joints around. What's romantic about that? You and your honey get to feel like chaperons at the junior high dance. No gloating, please. 🕐 *At least 10 min. Zero Post Office Sq.* ☎ *617/ 423-1500. www.posquare.com. T: Blue or Orange Line to State.*

⑥ ★★ Milk Street Cafe. Post Office Square Park is home to this top-notch purveyor of soups, salads, sandwiches, and sweets. You'd never know unless someone told you, but it's all kosher. *Post Office Square Park.* ☎ *617/542-3663. $–$$.*

⑦ ★ Province Street. A side street on the edge of a downtown business district might not seem promising for romance, but push on. In the 1820s, this was a posh residential neighborhood. On the same side of the street as the garage is a short stone wall topped by a metal fence with a fancy gate in the middle. The gate sits at the bottom of a short flight of stone stairs—a perfect place to steal a kiss. *Province St. at Bosworth St. (between Bromfield and School sts.)*

⑧ ★★★ Otis House Museum. One of New England's most famous architects, Charles Bulfinch, made his name by popularizing the Federal style in residences as well as public spaces that survive to this day (including the Massachusetts State House). This magnificent home, completed in 1796, was the first of three he designed for his friend Harrison Gray Otis. The engrossing tour touches on the history of the neighborhood, discusses historic preservation, and, most important, shows off the house and its furnishings. As interesting as the architectural details are, they share the spotlight with the story of a companionable young family bound for bigger things. Otis, a real estate developer who was later a congressman and mayor of Boston, and his wife, Sally Foster Otis, appointed their home in grand style and enjoyed a reputation for

The winding streets of Beacon Hill are the perfect place for a romantic stroll.

Salt and Pepper Bridge (aka Longfellow Bridge), with its namesake towers.

entertaining lavishly. They were married for nearly 50 years. *141 Cambridge St. (Staniford St.); enter from Lynde St.* ☎ *617/227-3956. www.historicnewengland.org. Tours $8. Tours on the hour and half-hour Wed–Sun 11am–4:30pm. T: Green or Blue Line to Government Center (or Blue Line to Bowdoin, on weekdays only).*

9 ★★ **Charles Street.** One of the best streets in the entire city for aimless strolling, Charles Street abounds with gift and antiques shops. It's also the heart of this little residential area, with such nontouristy businesses as a pharmacy and a convenience store (the 7-Eleven at 66 Charles St., with hilariously low-key signage that follows the street's strict zoning rules). See chapter 4 for shopping tips, or just wander around. *Cambridge St. to Beacon St. T: Red Line to Charles/ MGH.*

10 ★ **Panificio.** Superb fresh breads, pastries, sandwiches, and pizza will draw you to this little storefront restaurant. The cozy atmosphere will keep you here for a while. *144 Charles St. (Revere and Cambridge sts.).* ☎ *227-4340. $–$$.*

11 ★★ **Longfellow Bridge.** Originally the West Boston Bridge, this bridge is nicknamed the Salt and Pepper Bridge, because the towers resemble salt and pepper shakers. It's my favorite for the up-close views of the Charles River Basin, the straight-down views of Boston Duck Tours vehicles and sailboats, and the distant views of the setting sun. (And if your timing is exactly right, the rising moon appears to float in the John Hancock Tower.) Most important, the sidewalks on either side of the busy road split briefly so pedestrians can pass around the ornate towers. On the water side of these little recesses, you can take in the panorama and snuggle with your sweetie. *Between the intersection of Cambridge and Charles sts., Boston, and the intersection of Main St. and Memorial Dr., Cambridge.*

Tying the **Freedom Trail** Together

1. Boston Common
2. Robert Gould Shaw Memorial
3. Massachusetts State House
4. Park Street Church
5. Old Granary Burying Ground
6. King's Chapel & Burying Ground
7. First Public School / Benjamin Franklin Statue
8. Old Corner Bookstore Building
9. Old South Meeting House
10. Old State House
11. Boston Massacre Site
12. Faneuil Hall
13. Faneuil Hall Marketplace
14. The New England Holocaust Memorial
15. Paul Revere House
16. Mike's Pastry
17. James Rego Square (Paul Revere Mall)
18. Old North Church
19. Copp's Hill Burying Ground
20. USS *Constitution*
21. USS *Constitution* Museum
22. Bunker Hill Monument
23. Sorelle

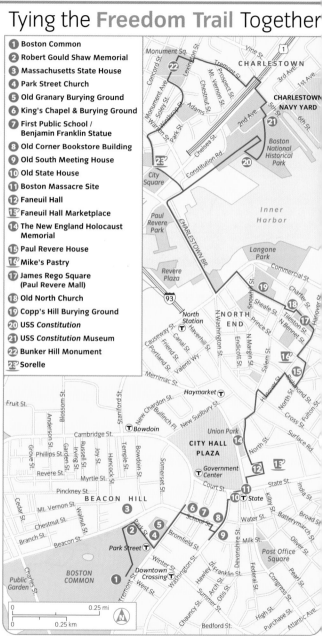

A reminder: The Freedom Trail is a suggested route. People constantly tell me they're curious about the rest of downtown Boston, but they don't want to get lost. They're afraid to start at the end of the trail, skip a stop or two, and generally personalize the experience. But Boston is *tiny*. No matter how far you wander, you can't get very lost. To emphasize how modular the trail can be—if you're willing to approach it that way—I've scattered the descriptions of many of the stops throughout the rest of this book. If you're determined to "do" the trail in order, allow at least 4 hours, and be prepared to incorporate a serendipitous detour or two. Now that we're clear on that, here's the Freedom Trail, in the usual order.

START: **Red or Green Line to Park St.**

1 ★ **Boston Common.** See p 7, bullet **1**.

2 ★★★ **Robert Gould Shaw Memorial.** See p 7, bullet **2**.

3 ★ **Massachusetts State House.** At the back of the building (off Bowdoin St.), check out the column topped by an eagle. It's 60 feet (18m) tall, representing the original height of Beacon Hill before earth that from the top went into 19th-century landfill projects. See p 7, bullet **3**.

4 **Park Street Church.** The plaques across the front of this striking building describe significant events in its history. Most Bostonians know the church for its 217-foot (66m) clock tower and steeple. *1 Park St. (Tremont St.)* 617/523-3383. www.parkstreet.org. Tours July–Aug Tues–Sat 9:30am–3:30pm. T: Red or Green Line to Park St.

5 ★★ **Old Granary Burying Ground.** See p 7, bullet **4**.

6 ★ **King's Chapel and Burying Ground.** My favorite thing about this church is the method of construction: The granite building went up

Freedom Trail marker.

around its wooden predecessor, which remained in use. See p 97, bullet **2**.

7 **First Public School/Benjamin Franklin Statue.** The Benjamin Franklin Statue sits behind the fence that surrounds Old City Hall. The colorful sidewalk mosaic out front marks the site of the first public school in the United States. See p 8, bullet **6**.

8 **Old Corner Bookstore Building.** This land once belonged to religious reformer Anne Hutchinson, who was excommunicated and banished from Massachusetts for heresy in 1638. The current structure dates to around 1712. It's best known today as the one-time home of Ticknor & Fields, publisher of some such authors as Longfellow, Emerson, Thoreau, Alcott, and Stowe. Step across the street and take a moment to appreciate the scale and the very existence of this building, which was already old when the American Revolution was just breaking out. *285 Washington St. (School St.)*

9 ★ **kids** **Old South Meeting House.** The Boston Tea Party, one of the pivotal political demonstrations of the pre-Revolutionary era, started here in 1773. The displays and exhibits in the one-time house of worship—now used for lectures, concerts, and other events—tell the story in a low-key yet compelling fashion. *A tip:* As you leave, look across the street at 1 Milk Street, an office building standing roughly where 17 Milk Street was in 1706, when Benjamin Franklin was born there. The facade incorporates a bust of Ben and the words BIRTHPLACE OF FRANKLIN. *310 Washington St. (Milk St.)* ☎ *617/482-6439. www.oldsouth-meetinghouse.org. Admission $5 adults, $4 seniors and students, $1 kids 6–18, free for kids under 6. Daily Apr–Oct 9:30am–5pm; Nov–Mar 10am–4pm. T: Blue or Orange Line to State.*

🔟 ★ kids **Old State House.** See p 8, bullet ⑦.

⓫ **Boston Massacre Site.** A circle of cobblestones embedded in a traffic island honors the five men killed by British troops on March 5, 1770. A marker on the Devonshire Street side of the Old State House (all the way over by the curb—it's easy to miss) tells the story. *State St. at Devonshire St.*

⓬ ★ kids **Faneuil Hall.** See p 9, bullet ⑧.

Six million numbers are etched into the Holocaust memorial's six glass towers, representing the 6 million Jews who died.

⓭ ★★ kids **Faneuil Hall Marketplace.** See p 9, bullet ⑨.

⓮ ★★ kids **The New England Holocaust Memorial.** This memorial isn't formally part of the Freedom Trail. I always include it, though—when we think about freedom, it's important to contemplate the consequences of having it taken away. *Union St. (North and Hanover sts.)* ☎ *617/457-8755. www.nehm.org. T: Orange or Green Line to Haymarket.*

⓯ ★★★ kids **Paul Revere House.** See p 11, bullet ⑪.

⓰ ★★ **Mike's Pastry.** Italian pastries are always a good idea. So are all-American treats such as brownies and chocolate chip cookies. *300 Hanover St. (Prince St.)* ☎ *617/742-3050. $.*

⓱ ★ **James Rego Square (Paul Revere Mall).** Be sure to check out the left-hand wall of this square, which holds numerous tablets that describe important people and places in the history of the North End. *Off Hanover St. (Clark St.)*

⓲ ★★ **Old North Church.** See p 52, bullet ⑥.

⓳ ★ **Copp's Hill Burying Ground.** See p 98, bullet ④.

⓴ ★★ kids **USS *Constitution*.** See p 57, bullet ②.

㉑ ★ kids **USS *Constitution* Museum.** See p 58, bullet ③.

㉒ ★ **Bunker Hill Monument.** See p 59, bullet ⑥.

㉓ ★ **Sorelle.** Pastries, sandwiches, and salads served in a sleek contemporary space make a good transition from your Colonial excursion back to real life. *100 City Sq. (Chelsea St.).* ☎ *617/242-5980. $–$$.* ●

3 The Best
Neighborhood Tours

Beacon Hill

1 Massachusetts State House
2 Nichols House Museum
3 Louisburg Square
4 Acorn Street
5 Charles Street
6 Café Vanille
7 Myrtle Street Playground
8 Museum of Afro-American History
9 Café Podima

The views are better from the waterfront, the real estate is more expensive in the Back Bay, but the most prestigious addresses in Boston are on beautiful Beacon Hill, as they have been for most of the past 2 centuries. Post-Revolution prosperity created Boston's most prominent (in all senses of the word) neighborhood, which is a visual treat from all angles. Wear comfortable shoes.

START: **Red or Green Line to Park Street**

① ★ **Massachusetts State House.** The construction of the state capitol, which opened in 1798, coincided with Beacon Hill becoming a fashionable neighborhood. Before the Revolution, most Bostonians lived in the area around what are now Faneuil Hall Marketplace and the North End; with peace and increasing prosperity, the population ballooned and construction boomed. The prototypical Boston building, of red brick with white marble trim, owes its iconic status to one man: Charles Bulfinch. The best-known architect of the Federal era (1780–1820), Bulfinch designed the golden-domed central building of the State House as well as many of the graceful residences you'll see on this tour. See p 7, bullet ③.

The Massachusetts State House.

② ★ **Nichols House Museum.** In contrast to the adjacent Back Bay, where many historic structures hold offices, schools, condos, and apartments, Beacon Hill retains a fair number of one-family homes (along with plenty of condos and apartments). Almost all of the private residences on the narrow streets of "the Hill" are tantalizingly close yet inaccessible to visitors. This 1804 building, which is attributed to Charles Bulfinch, is a welcome exception. It permits a glimpse of life during the lifetime of the house's most famous occupant, Rose Standish Nichols (1872–1960). "Miss Rose" was a suffragist, feminist, pacifist, and pioneering landscape designer. She traveled all over the world, returning home with much of the art and artifacts that decorate her house, which became a museum after her death. Most of the furnishings in the four-story building are gorgeous antiques collected by several generations of the Nichols family, who moved here in 1885, not long before the novelist Henry James called Mount Vernon Street "the only respectable street in America." ⏱ *45 min. 55 Mount Vernon St. (Joy and Walnut sts.)* ☎ *617/227-6993. www.nicholshousemuseum.org. Admission $7. May–Oct Tues–Sat noon–4pm, Nov–Apr Thurs–Sat noon–4pm; tours every 30 min. Open days may vary, so call ahead. T: Red or Green Line to Park St.*

③ ★★★ **Louisburg Square.** The fanciest addresses in Boston's fanciest neighborhood surround the namesake park—pronounced "lewis-burg"—which sits within a daunting iron fence. The architecture is consistent yet random, employing the same materials in a pleasing variety of styles. Take some time to circle the square. ⏱ *20 min. Between Mount Vernon St. (at Willow St.) and Pinckney St. (at Grove St.)*

Louisburg Square

Pinckney Street

Louisburg Square

Mount Vernon Street

An Italian marble likeness of Athenian statesman **3A Aristides** anchors one end of the private park, which is the common property of the Louisburg Square Proprietors. The organization is believed to be the oldest homeowners' association in the country. The 22 houses that surround the graceful patch of grass and trees were built between 1834 and 1848; Aristides landed here in 1850. Not so long ago, lingering in front of **3B 19 Louisburg Square** would have earned you a chat with a Secret Service agent. U.S. senator John Kerry, the 2004 Democratic presidential candidate, lives here (and in a number of other swanky places) with his wife, Teresa Heinz Kerry. The rendering of

3C Christopher Columbus at this stop is believed to be the first American statue honoring Columbus. Use him as an excuse to peer inside the fence. The celebrated 19th-century singer Jenny Lind—promoted as the "Swedish Nightingale" by impresario P. T. Barnum—married her accompanist in the parlor of the house at **3D 20 Louisburg Square** in 1852. Beloved author Louisa May Alcott bought the house at **3E 10 Louisburg Square** in 1885, but she lived here for only about 3 years. She had contracted mercury poisoning while serving as a nurse during the Civil War, and her health was failing. In 1888, on the day after her father's funeral, Alcott died here.

Homes in Beacon Hill's exclusive Louisburg Square.

④ Acorn Street. This adorable cobblestone thoroughfare feels like a surprise. It's something of an open secret to clued-in Bostonians—and no secret at all to postcard photographers. You'll see why when you get there. *Between Willow and W. Cedar sts.*

⑤ ★★ Charles Street. Look past the signs and merchandise to appreciate the structural details of the 19th-century buildings that line Beacon Hill's main commercial street. This might be the most enjoyable area in the city in which to wander. ⏱ *At least 30 min. See p 41, bullet* **⑨**.

⑥ ★★ Café Vanille. One of the best French bakeries in the city, Café Vanille is a perfect place to relax with a pastry or sandwich and a cup of strong coffee. Watch out for the smokers who take over the outdoor seating area. *70 Charles St.* ☎ *617/523-9200. $.*

⑦ Myrtle Street Playground. Climbing all over Beacon Hill is no holiday for your legs; give them a rest at this delightful little oasis. *S. Russell and Irving sts.*

⑧ ★★ Museum of Afro-American History. This fascinating museum offers visitors a comprehensive look at the history and contributions of blacks in Boston and Massachusetts. It occupies the Abiel Smith School (1834), the first American public grammar school for African-American children, and the African Meeting House (1806), one of the oldest black churches in the country. Changing and permanent exhibits use art, artifacts, documents, historic photographs, and other objects to explore an important era that often takes a back seat in Revolutionary War–obsessed New England. Don't leave without venturing down Holmes Alley, off Smith Court—the narrow passageway is believed to have been a hiding place for fugitive slaves traveling the Underground Railroad. ⏱ *1 hr. 46 Joy St. (Myrtle and Cambridge sts.).* ☎ *617/725-0022. www.afroammuseum.org. Free admission; donations encouraged. Mon–Sat 10am–4pm. T: Red or Green Line to Park St.*

⑨ Café Podima. Students from nearby Suffolk University flock here, drawn by the large portions and low prices. Have a salad, sandwich, or pizza, or just grab some ice cream or frozen yogurt. *168 Cambridge St.* ☎ *617/227-4959. $.*

Indulge in a decadent French pastry at Café Vanille.

The North End

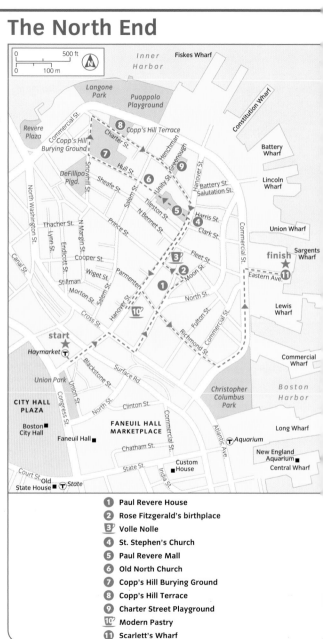

1. Paul Revere House
2. Rose Fitzgerald's birthplace
3. Volle Nolle
4. St. Stephen's Church
5. Paul Revere Mall
6. Old North Church
7. Copp's Hill Burying Ground
8. Copp's Hill Terrace
9. Charter Street Playground
10. Modern Pastry
11. Scarlett's Wharf

Boston's best-known Italian-American neighborhood is in transition, but it's still the area's top destination for pasta, cappuccino, pastries, and the lively street life that makes this crowded, friendly area endlessly appealing to pedestrians. As you wander around, remember to look up—among the architectural flourishes executed by the talented craftsmen who worked on many of the buildings, you may see a *nonna* (grandma) looking out the window, keeping track of the action on her street. START: **Green or Orange Line to Haymarket**

1 ★★★ kids Paul Revere House. With its good water supply and easy access to the harbor, the North End was one of the first areas of Boston settled by Europeans. The Paul Revere House, the oldest surviving house downtown, was built around 1680, in the wake of a huge fire in 1676. See p 11, bullet **11**.

2 Rose Fitzgerald's birthplace. A plaque marks the modest tenement building where President John Fitzgerald Kennedy's mother came into the world in 1890. It recalls the days when the North End was an Irish and Jewish neighborhood. For much of the 20th century, the North End was Boston's best-known Italian-American area; today the neighborhood is estimated to

be less than half Italian-American, having become popular with young professionals who walk to work downtown and, relatively recently, empty nesters fleeing the suburbs. *4 Garden Court at Prince St.*

3 ★★ kids Volle Nolle. An up-and-coming neighborhood favorite for sophisticated sandwiches and scrumptious baked goods, Volle Nolle isn't a typical North End sub shop—and that's a good thing. *351 Hanover St. (Fleet St.)* ☎ *617/523-0003. $.*

4 ★ St. Stephen's Church. St. Stephen's, one of three Roman Catholic houses of worship in the

Paul Revere made his living as a silversmith, but he made his reputation as an equestrian.

You can snap your own version of this shot, one of Boston's best photo ops, on the Paul Revere Mall.

tiny North End, is the only standing church building in Boston designed by Charles Bulfinch. The design bears the hallmarks the architect's iconic style, including the symmetry that makes Federal architecture so pleasing to the eye—step across the street to appreciate it fully. At its dedication in 1804, St. Stephen's was Unitarian; it changed with the neighborhood's population and became Catholic in 1862. A refurbishment in 1965 restored the building's original austere details, including clear (not stained) glass windows. The bell, installed in 1805, came from Paul Revere's foundry and cost the congregation $800. Rose Fitzgerald (later Rose Kennedy) was baptized here in 1890, and her funeral took place here in 1995. ⏱ *10 min. 401 Hanover St. (Clark St.)*

⑤ ★ Paul Revere Mall. Also known as James Rego Square but usually just called the Prado, this tree-shaded plaza links the commotion of Hanover Street and the serenity of the Old North Church. One of the best photo ops in the city is here: Focus on the equestrian statue of Paul Revere, then allow the church steeple to stray into the frame. The

sculptor was Cyrus Dallin, who also created the Indian on horseback in front of the Museum of Fine Arts. Wander slowly here, taking time to peruse the plaques that line the left-hand wall; they commemorate important people and places in the history of the neighborhood. *Hanover St. (Clark and Harris sts.)*

⑥ ★ Old North Church (Christ Church). This beautifully proportioned brick church, designed in the style of Sir Christopher Wren, fairly overflows with historic associations. It contains the oldest American church bells (cast in Gloucester, England, and installed in 1745), the Revere family's pew, and a bust of George Washington that's believed to be the first memorial to the first president. The strongest link is with Paul Revere, who arranged for sexton Robert Newman to hang two lanterns in the steeple on the night of April 18, 1775, signaling to the rebellious colonists that British troops were leaving Boston by water ("two if by sea"), bound for Lexington and Concord. The original weather vane tops the current

Old North Church, the oldest church building in Boston, dates to 1723.

steeple, the church's third, which is a replica of the original. The behind-the-scenes tour takes visitors up into the spire and down to the crypt. It's definitely not for the claustrophobic, but irresistible for those who are curious about colonial times. My favorite feature of the church isn't actually in the church—it's the tranquil gardens on the north side of the building (to the left as you face the main entrance from the street). ⏱ 40 min. 193 Salem St. ☎ 617/523-6676. www.oldnorth.com. $3 donation requested. Free tours every 15 min. Behind-the-scenes tour $8 adults, $5 kids under 17; available June to mid-Aug weekend afternoons and weekdays, rest of the year by appointment. Reservations recommended. Daily 9am–5pm. T: Orange or Green Line to Haymarket.

⑦ ★ Copp's Hill Burying Ground. The highest point in the North End affords a panoramic view across the Inner Harbor to the Charlestown Navy Yard, where the three masts of USS Constitution poke into view. "Old Ironsides" was built near here, at Hartt's Shipyard at what's now 409 Commercial Street, and launched in 1797. *Fun fact:* The 10-foot-wide (3m) private home at 44 Hull Street, across the street from the Copp's Hill entrance, is the narrowest house in Boston. See p 98, bullet ④.

⑧ ★★ Copp's Hill Terrace. Because the back gate of the burying ground is always locked, you'll have to walk all the way around to get to this little plaza. The seating area, on a patch of concrete that overlooks a terraced lawn, has a great view of the action on the athletic fields across the street and the harbor and Charlestown Navy Yard beyond. Commercial Street, directly below, was the location of one of the weirdest disasters ever, in this or any other city: the molasses flood of January 1919. A 2.3-million-gallon industrial storage tank blew apart, sending

thousands of tons of molasses pouring through the streets, killing 21 people and injuring dozens more. *Charter St. (Snowhill and Foster sts.)*

⑨ ★ Charter Street Playground. Seek out this pocket park tucked between the tourist tracks of the Freedom Trail and Hanover Street, and you'll be the only out-of-towner who's here intentionally. The little patch of greenery and cobblestones is home to a sweet sculpture of a seal. *Greenough Lane, off Charter St. at Unity St.*

⑩ ★★ Modern Pastry. Load up on cookies or pastries (ask for a fork if you order something messy, like the sublime tiramisu) and head toward the water for a mini-picnic overlooking the harbor. *257 Hanover St.* ☎ 617/523-3783. *$.*

⑪ ★ Scarlett's Wharf. The little park at the end of the wharf behind the parking lot is a neighborhood secret—it's not visible from the street, but it hums with activity. The free telescopes allow views of the maritime traffic on the Inner Harbor and the action at the airport, which feels close enough to touch. *Off Commercial St. at Eastern Ave. (north side of 2 Atlantic Ave.)*

Copp's Hill Burying Ground.

The Waterfront

Commercial Wharf

Christopher Columbus Park

Richmond St.
Fulton St.
Commercial St.
Cross St.
Atlantic Ave.
Commercial St.

start
★ Ⓣ *Aquarium*

Long Wharf ❶

State St.
Custom House ■
Central St.
Surface Rd.
India St.
Milk St.
Well St.
Broad St.
Batterymarch St.
Franklin St.
High St.
Oliver St.
Pearl St.
Purchase St.

❷ Central Wharf

India Wharf

B o s t o n

H a r b o r

Rowes Wharf

❸

NORTHERN AVE. BR.
❹
Fan Pier

Independence Wharf ■
EVELYN MOAKLEY BR.
finish
★ 🅶 ❺

Atlantic Ave.

Ft. Point Channel

Seeger St.
Congress St.
Federal Reserve Plaza ■
Farnsworth St.
Thomson St.
Seaport Blvd
Northern Ave

Boston Tea Party Ship & Museum ■
❻
CONGRESS ST. BR.
Dorchester Ave
SUMMER ST. BR.
Summer St.
Boston Wharf Rd.

❶ Long Wharf Plaza
❷ New England Aquarium
❸ Rowes Wharf
❹ Old Northern Avenue Bridge
❺ Moakley Federal Courthouse
❻ Boston Children's Museum
🅶 The Barking Crab

Boston is a thoroughly modern city, and its commerce and conveniences sometimes make it feel interchangeable with any other good-sized municipality. Then the wind shifts and tangy sea air pours in from the east, a powerful reminder that you're visiting a legendary seaport. Stroll along the harbor to experience Boston's shoreline—and that infamous east wind. START: **Blue Line to Aquarium**

1 ★★ Long Wharf Plaza. Not quite a park, hardly a famous attraction, this little peninsula is one of my favorite places in Boston. **A tip:** In the summer, check the time the full moon rises, and be here to watch—you'll never forget it. See p 39, bullet **1**.

2 ★ kids New England Aquarium. See p 22, bullet **4**.

3 ★★ Rowes Wharf. The Chicago firm of Skidmore, Owings & Merrill designed this hotel-office-retail-residential complex, which opened in 1987 and centers on a landmark archway. Walk along the water to fully appreciate Rowes Wharf's brilliant combination of private development and public access. *Atlantic Ave. at High St., near Northern Ave.*

4 ★ Old Northern Avenue Bridge. Completed in 1908, this is an iron-turntable or "swing" bridge that opens by rotating on a pivot rather than by lifting up like a drawbridge. Well, *opened*—the adjacent Evelyn Moakley Bridge (1996) made it obsolete, but public protests have saved the deteriorating old bridge, which is now pedestrian only, from demolition several times. *Old Northern Ave. (Atlantic Ave. and Sleeper St.)*

5 ★★ Moakley Federal Courthouse. The South Boston Waterfront, also known as the Seaport District, has grown in fits and starts over the past decade or so. A milestone was the 1998 opening of this glorious building, formally the John Joseph Moakley United States Courthouse. Does the boring brick facade make you wonder what I think "glorious" means? Walk around to the water side. The heart of Henry Cobb's design is the glass wall that allows panoramic harbor views from inside. The public is welcome to check out a trial or even grab a bite in the cafeteria (the guards in the lobby will confiscate your cellphone). *1 Courthouse Way (Seaport Blvd. at Sleeper St.)* ☎ *617/748-9057 (clerk's office). Mon–Fri 8am–6pm. T: Silver Line bus from South Station.*

6 ★★ kids Boston Children's Museum. See p 23, bullet **5**.

7 ★ kids The Barking Crab. Grab a seat on the deck of this colorful crab shack overlooking the Fort Point Channel (which separates downtown from South Boston), sip a beer, and snack on some fresh seafood. *88 Sleeper St. (Northern Ave.).* ☎ *617/426-2722. $$–$$$.*

Ferries lining up along Long Wharf Plaza.

Charlestown

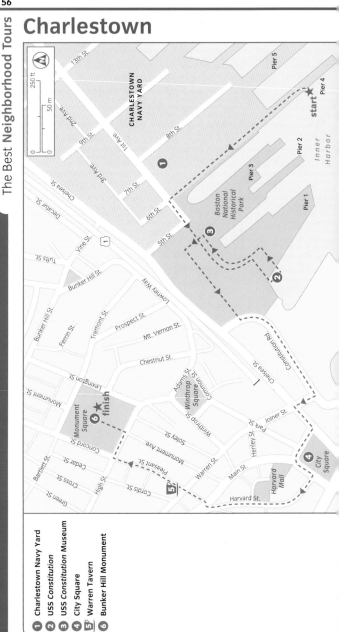

1 Charlestown Navy Yard
2 USS Constitution
3 USS Constitution Museum
4 City Square
5 Warren Tavern
6 Bunker Hill Monument

Charlestown, the neighborhood across the Inner Harbor from the North End, was originally settled as a separate town in 1629 (a year before Boston proper). It became part of the city in 1874 but retains an air of individuality—and a reputation for insularity that's slowly yielding to gentrification. START: **Ferry from Long Wharf (Blue Line T to Aquarium) to Charlestown Navy Yard**

① Charlestown Navy Yard. The shipyard built, supplied, and maintained U.S. Navy vessels from 1800 to 1974. At its height, during World War II, the facility employed more than 40,000 people. Although it's no longer an active base, it's home to one of the most famous ships in the history of the United States, USS *Constitution*. The navy yard combines residential, office, and lab space with military monuments, explanatory plaques galore, and a 30-acre (12ha) piece of the Boston National Historical Park. Take a ranger-guided tour if you're so inclined, but thanks to all the plaques you can do just as well wandering on your own. ⏲ *15 min. to explore independently; 1 hr. for*

Old Ironsides.

ranger tour. Off Chelsea St.; enter through Gate 1, at Constitution Rd. ☎ *617/242-5601. www.nps.gov/bost. Daily 9am–5pm. Call ahead if the national terror alert level rises; the navy yard may close for security reasons. Free admission. T: Ferry from Long Wharf, or Green or Orange Line to North Station and 10-min. walk.*

② ★★ kids USS *Constitution*. The three masts of this mighty frigate loom over the navy yard, and the gorgeous black hull is one of the most eye-catching sights on the harbor. On August 19, 1812, during an engagement with HMS *Guerriere* during the War of 1812, the British vessel's cannonballs bounced off the *Constitution*'s thick oak hull as if it were iron, and the nickname "Old Ironsides" was born. The oldest commissioned floating warship in the world (launched in 1797 and retired in 1815), Old Ironsides never lost a battle, but narrowly escaped destruction several times in its first 2 centuries. Today the 204-foot-long (62m) ship is a beloved symbol of Boston. Visiting is a bit of a pain; this is an active-duty posting for the sailors who lead the tours (outfitted in fancy-pants 1812 dress uniforms), and security is tight. The tour—a fascinating overview as well as a great opportunity to mingle with people from all over the country and around the world—is worth the trouble. ⏲ *1 hr., including security screening; arrive as early as possible to beat the tour groups. Charlestown Navy Yard.* ☎ *617/242-7511. www.uss constitution.navy.mil. Free admission. Summer Tues–Sun 10am–6pm; tours*

Quincy Market architect Alexander Parris also designed the USS Constitution *museum building.*

every 30 min. until 3:30pm. Winter Thurs–Sun 10am–4pm; tours every 30 min. until 3:30pm. T: Ferry from Long Wharf, or Green or Orange Line to North Station and 10-min. walk.

3 ★ kids USS *Constitution* Museum. The *Constitution* is, for the most part, a hands-off experience; its museum is exactly the opposite. Children (and adults) push buttons, open doors, pull ropes, study artifacts, watch demonstrations of maritime crafts, and enjoy the interactive exhibits. The granite building was originally the navy yard's wood and metal shop.
⏱: 30 min. Building 22, off First Ave. ☎ 617/426-1812. www.uss constitutionmuseum.org. Free admission; donations encouraged. Daily May–Oct 15 9am–6pm; Oct 16–Apr 10am–5pm. T: Ferry from Long Wharf, or Green or Orange Line to North Station and 10-min. walk.

4 ★ City Square. Not so long ago, this was a grim patch of asphalt crouching beneath a hideous highway overpass. Today it's one of the most pleasant side effects of the Big Dig, the highway-construction project that took over Boston in the 1990s. The center-piece is City Square Park, a 1-acre (.4ha) oasis of lawns, trees, shrubs, flowers, and benches, dotted with plaques and memorials and graced with a fountain. After the highway was moved underground, the park opened in 1996, foreshadowing the explosion of public outdoor space that followed the completion of the downtown sections of the Big Dig. Note the sculptures of creatures around the park; they include a crane at the top of the fountain (the Three Cranes Tavern once stood on this site) and numerous cod that honor the integral role the fish once played in Boston's economy. *Rutherford Ave. and Chelsea St.*

5 ★ **Warren Tavern.** The British torched Charlestown as they left in 1775, destroying most of its pre-Revolutionary buildings. This wooden structure, completed around 1780, was part of the wave of construction that followed. It's an excellent place for a bite and a break. *2 Pleasant St. (Main St.)* ☎ *617/241-8142. $–$$.*

6 ★ **Bunker Hill Monument.** The narrow streets of Charlestown all seem to lead to this elegant square. The 221-foot (67m) obelisk at the center commemorates the Battle of Bunker Hill on June 17, 1775; to this day, June 17 is Bunker Hill Day, a holiday in Suffolk County. The British won that battle, but nearly half of their troops were killed or wounded. Partly as a consequence of the carnage, the royal troops abandoned Boston 9 months later (on March 17, also a local holiday, Evacuation Day). The exhibits in the lodge at the base of the granite monument, designed by the prolific Solomon Willard, tell the story of the battle. Think hard before attempting the 294 stairs to the top; the climb is tough, and it ends at a small space with frustratingly tiny windows. I've done it once, and today when I find myself here with people who insist on heading up, I take advantage of the chance to wander the perimeter of the square and check out the pleasantly diverse architecture. A bit of trivia: The Battle of Bunker Hill was actually fought on Breed's Hill; you're there. ⏱ *30 min. if you stay on the ground; 1 hr. if you climb the stairs. Monument Sq. at Monument Ave.* ☎ *617/242-5641. www.nps.gov/bost. Free admission. Exhibits daily 9am–5pm; monument daily 9am–4:30pm. T: Orange Line to Community College.*

Statue of William Prescott, who gave the legendary command: "Don't fire until you see the whites of their eyes."

Harvard Square

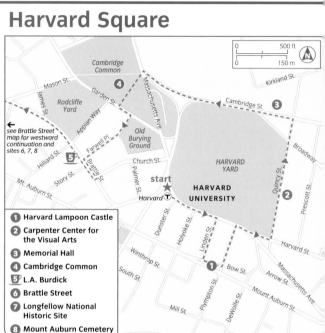

1. Harvard Lampoon Castle
2. Carpenter Center for the Visual Arts
3. Memorial Hall
4. Cambridge Common
5. L.A. Burdick
6. Brattle Street
7. Longfellow National Historic Site
8. Mount Auburn Cemetery

Much of the interesting architecture in and around Harvard Square is on the main Harvard University campus, and a great deal of it isn't. This tour touches on both. The school and "the Square" have been inextricably linked since they were just starting out—in the 1630s. Neither would be what it is today without the other. START: **Red Line to Harvard**

1 ★ **Harvard Lampoon Castle.** A peerless blend of form and function, the Harvard Lampoon Castle is the home of the university's best-known undergraduate humor magazine. The triangular building is suitably madcap, with colorful trim all around and a "face" of three windows and a door on the Linden Street end. The 1909 structure is the work of Edmund Wheelwright of the Boston firm of Wheelwright & Haven, also the architect of the Longfellow Bridge and numerous cultural venues. The *Lampoon* is a

legendary launching pad—the founders of the *National Lampoon* and dozens of writers for *Saturday Night Live, The Simpsons, Late Night with Conan O'Brien,* and other TV hits (and misses) got their start here.*57 Mount Auburn St. and 44 Bow St. (Linden and Plympton sts.)*

2 ★★ **Carpenter Center for the Visual Arts.** Completed in 1963, the Carpenter Center is the only North American building designed by the Swiss-French architect Le Corbusier. The concrete

John Harvard statue in Harvard Yard.

building's dynamic design encourages visitors to circulate on ramps that allow views of studio space from the public areas. The university's Visual and Environmental Studies department and the Harvard Film Archive make their homes here, and the two gallery spaces are open to the public. Purists deplore the way the Carpenter Center relates to its surroundings; pause across the street to contemplate the site, which does seem to cramp the building's style, even to the amateur's eye. *24 Quincy St. (Harvard St. and Broadway).* ☎ *617/495-3251. Mon–Sat 9am–11:30pm, Sun noon–11:30pm.*

❸ ★ **Memorial Hall.** The architects of "Mem Hall," the firm of Ware & Van Brunt, won a design competition that was open only to Harvard graduates (who wonder why people think they're snobs). The cornerstone was laid in 1870 and construction completed in 1875. See p 18, bullet ❻.

❹ ★ **Cambridge Common.** Set aside as common land in 1631, just a year after the founding of Cambridge (then called Newtowne), the Common sometimes feels like the one of the only quiet parts of Harvard Square. Legend has it that George Washington took control of the Continental Army here in July 1775, but historians have debunked the specifics of the story. Nevertheless, a memorial surrounded by three cannons commemorates the event. A more interesting marker is on the edge of the Common. While Paul Revere was leaving Boston by boat on the night of April 18, 1775, William Dawes slipped out of town on the narrow causeway where present-day Washington Street enters the South End. Both riders headed for Lexington and Concord, and Dawes's route took him through the heart of Cambridge. On Massachusetts Avenue just north of Garden Street, horseshoes embedded in the sidewalk illustrate his path. *Massachusetts Ave. and Garden St.*

❺ ☕ ★★ **L. A. Burdick.** The cafe—one of only a handful of retail locations operated by the celebrated New Hampshire–based confectioner—serves and sells candy, pastries, and drinks. *52-D Brattle St.* ☎ *617/491-4340. $–$$.*

Memorial Hall.

6 ★★★ **Brattle Street.** One of the most beautiful residential streets in the country, Brattle Street has been an exclusive address for over 2 centuries. It gained fame—and the nickname "Tory Row"—around the time of the Revolution because of its association with British sympathizers. The loyalists wound up evacuating, but some of their lovely homes survive.

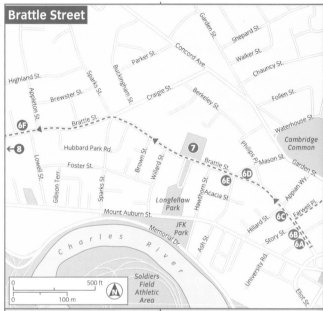

Brattle Street

The 1727 **6A William Brattle House** (no. 42) is the property of the nonprofit Cambridge Center for Adult Education. A splash of modern design in Colonial Cambridge, the 1969 **6B Design Research Building** (no. 48) is the work of Benjamin Thompson and Associates. It houses a branch of Crate & Barrel. The Cambridge Center for Adult Education also owns the **6C Hancock-Dexter-Pratt House** (no. 54), constructed in 1811 and immortalized by Longfellow, who saw the village blacksmith working here in the late 1830s. There's a pleasant cafe on the first floor (see p 37, bullet **9**). The 1847 Gothic Revival **6D Burleigh House** is also known as the Norton-Johnson-Burleigh House (no. 85). Our old friend H. H. Richardson designed the **6E Stoughton House** (no. 90), which was completed in 1883. The Cambridge Historical Society (☎ 617/547-4252; www.cambridgehistory.org) makes its home in the striking **6F Hooper-Lee-Nichols House** (no. 159), built around 1685 and substantially modified since then. The tour ($5 adults, $3 seniors and students) is interesting enough, but it's only offered Tuesday and Thursday at 2 and 3 pm. Don't knock yourself out to get here for it.

7 ★★ Longfellow National Historic Site. Henry Wadsworth Longfellow lived here from 1843 until his death, in 1882. He first made his home here as a boarder in 1837; after he married Fanny Appleton, her father made the house a wedding present. The current furnishings and books belonged to the poet and his descendants. The Vassall-Craigie-Longfellow House was built in 1759 and served as George Washington's headquarters in 1775 and 1776, during the siege of Boston; note the bust of the president at the bottom of the stairs in the first-floor entry hall. ⏱: *1 hr. 105 Brattle St. (Longfellow Park).* ☎ *617/491-1054. www.nps.gov/long. Apr–May Tues–Sat 10am–4:30pm, June–Oct Wed–Sun 10am–4:30pm; always check ahead. Tour $3 adults, free for kids under 17. T: Red Line to Harvard, 10-min. walk up Brattle St.*

8 ★★ Mount Auburn Cemetery. Consecrated in 1831, Mount Auburn was the first of the "garden cemeteries" that gained popularity as urban centers became too congested to support the expansion of downtown burying grounds. I find all cemeteries interesting; this one is a particularly fascinating combination of landscaping, statuary, sculpture, architecture, and, most important, history. It's possible to tour on foot or in a car, using a rented tape or CD.

One of Brattle Street's many elegant homes.

The notable people buried here range from Charles Bulfinch, who died in 1844, to Bernard Malamud, who died in 1986. They include Mary Baker Eddy, Isabella Stewart Gardner, Oliver Wendell Holmes, Julia Ward Howe, Winslow Homer, Henry Wadsworth Longfellow, and abolitionist Charles Sumner, among many others—and their numbers continue to grow. Bear in mind that Mount Auburn is an active cemetery: Animals and recreational activities (including picnicking and jogging) are forbidden. ⏱ *2 hr. 580 Mount Auburn St. (Brattle St. and Aberdeen Ave.).* ☎ *617/547-7105. www.mountauburn.org. Daily May–Sept 8am–7pm, Oct–Apr 8am–5pm. Tape or CD tour rental $7 ($15 deposit); available at entrance gate daily 8:30am–2pm. T: Red Line to Harvard, then bus no. 71 or 73.*

Mount Auburn's 175 acres (71ha) hold some 5,000 trees representing 700-plus species.

The South End

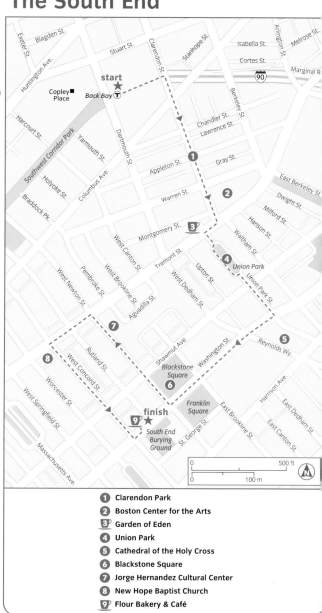

1. Clarendon Park
2. Boston Center for the Arts
3. Garden of Eden
4. Union Park
5. Cathedral of the Holy Cross
6. Blackstone Square
7. Jorge Hernandez Cultural Center
8. New Hope Baptist Church
9. Flour Bakery & Café

Long known as one of the city's most culturally and economically diverse neighborhoods, with a large gay community and an exciting restaurant scene, the sprawling South End gets yuppier by the day. Despite a lack of museums or other prominent attractions, its rewards are considerable for visitors who don't mind a fair amount of walking. START: **Orange Line to Back Bay**

❶ ★ **Clarendon Park.** South of Columbus Avenue, narrow, picturesque side streets make up the tiny enclave known as Clarendon Park. In either direction from Clarendon Street, little brick row houses with modest entrances and black-painted shutters line streets just wide enough to hold one lane of parking (a perennial scarcity in Boston) and one lane of traffic. The housing stock here recalls the mansions of Beacon Hill, but on a scale more accessible to the working people who made their homes in the South End before late-20th-century gentrification swept through. Today this is prime real estate. *Chandler, Lawrence, Appleton, and Gray sts. and Warren Ave. between Berkeley and Dartmouth sts.*

❷ ★★ **Boston Center for the Arts.** The Boston Center for the Arts, or BCA, is a 4-acre (7ha) complex of multiple performance spaces that centers on the Cyclorama. Regrettably not visible from the street, the circular Cyclorama—a huge enclosed space beneath a graceful 127-foot-wide (39m) dome—represents a popular form of 19th-century entertainment. Designed by Cummings and Sears and opened to the public in 1884, it originally held a panoramic painting, *The Battle of Gettysburg,* which was 50 feet (15m) tall and 400 feet (122m) long. As the popularity of cycloramas faded, the building became an entertainment venue, a boxing ring, an industrial site, and eventually the city's flower market. Redevelopment in the 1970s resulted in the return of the 23,000-square-foot (2,137sq. m) Cyclorama to its roots as an exhibition and performance space. If it's open to the public during your visit—I've been there for everything from a poetry reading to an antiques show—check it out. *539 Tremont St. (Clarendon and Berkeley sts.).* ☎ *617/426-7700 (events line). www.bcaonline.org.*

❸ **Garden of Eden.** Grab a sidewalk table, enjoy something tasty (from a snack to a sandwich to a comfort-food feast), and take in the neighborhood scene. *571 Tremont St. (Clarendon St.)* ☎ *617/247-8377. $–$$.*

❹ ★★ **Union Park.** One of the most beautiful spots in the entire city is this 1-block stretch of brick row houses surrounding an oval

Entrance to the BCA's Cyclorama.

Union Park. This square was laid out in the late 1850s.

park. Appealing architectural details abound, and an iron fence encloses the namesake park, which holds trees, flowers, lawns, and bubbling fountains. This was the first completed square in the rapidly developing neighborhood, which was then considered competition for the newly created Back Bay. The South End never quite gained the same cachet, however, and to this day—partly because public-transit access is better in the Back Bay—the younger area is ever-so-slightly pricier. *Tremont St. to Shawmut Ave.*

❺ ★ Cathedral of the Holy Cross. In Boston's early years, this was the site of the town gallows. The Puritan settlement wasn't exactly a magnet for Roman Catholics, but by the mid–19th century, the city's social and political climate had changed dramatically. The decade following the Civil War saw the construction of this edifice, which rivals Westminster Abbey in size. The building is 374 feet (114m) long and

seats more than 2,000. The Gothic Revival design is by the prolific Patrick Keely, an Irish immigrant who was reputedly the architect of more than 600 American houses of worship. Executed in Roxbury puddingstone, the plan originally called for a spire on each of the two towers, but they were never built. The elevated railway that ran along Washington Street for most of the 20th century did the cathedral no favors; the building and its stained-glass windows benefited considerably from the demolition of the "El," in 1987, and the resulting increased illumination. Most of the windows date to 1880, but my favorite is from 1940—a triptych in the south nave that depicts St. Fortunatus. It has so much going on that it almost appears to be moving. ⏱: *20 min. 1400 Washington St. (Union Park).* ☎ *617/542-5682. www.rcab.org.*

When it was consecrated in 1875, Holy Cross was the largest Catholic church in the United States.

Fountain in Blackstone Square.

6 ★★ Blackstone Square. The little park on your right is Blackstone Square; its sibling across Washington Street is Franklin Square. Charles Bulfinch planned this intersection in 1801, but his vision wasn't executed until the 1860s, when development was sweeping across the South End. Use your imagination to visualize this area as Bulfinch would have seen it, in the days when Washington Street was the primary land route to downtown Boston. Today, the twin green spaces represent a pleasant break from the man-made landscape of this built-up area; at the turn of the 19th century, they would have formed a stately entranceway to the city. *Washington St. (W. Brookline and W. Newton sts.)*

7 Jorge Hernández Cultural Center. A skillful restoration of a historic building, the cultural center occupies the former All Saints Lutheran Church. The German Gothic facade encloses a performance and event space that often books Latin musical artists and groups—quite a contrast for a place where Albert Schweitzer once played the organ. The 1899 church was falling apart when it was rehabbed in 1986, retaining a gorgeous stained-glass window; the adjacent parish house became La Casa de la Cultura/Center for Latino Arts, which holds an art gallery and studio space, after a \$1.3-million renovation in 2003. *85 W. Newton St. (Tremont St.)* ☎ *617/927-1737. www.claboston.org.*

8 ★ New Hope Baptist Church. Originally the Tremont Street Methodist Church, this 1862 Gothic Revival edifice is distinguished by the presence of two full-blown towers, one on either end. This was the first church in the Boston area constructed of Roxbury puddingstone, which later became a popular building material. The architect was Hammatt Billings, who earned his greatest fame as an illustrator. One of the best-known designers in Boston in the mid–19th century—when he created everything from fireworks displays to the original illustrations for *Uncle Tom's Cabin*—Billings is barely remembered today. *740 Tremont St. (W. Concord St.)* ☎ *617/536-9332. www.newhopians.org.*

9 ★ Flour Bakery & Cafe. Flour is a homey destination for all sorts of culinary delights, from a single superb cookie to a full meal. If they're available, don't miss the doughnuts. *1595 Washington St.* ☎ *617/267-4300. \$.*

Back Bay

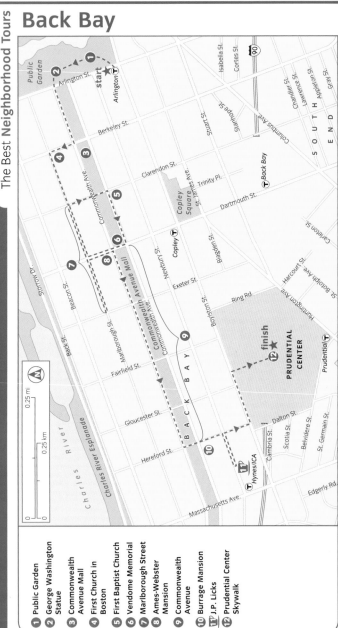

1 Public Garden
2 George Washington Statue
3 Commonwealth Avenue Mall
4 First Church in Boston
5 First Baptist Church
6 Vendome Memorial
7 Marlborough Street
8 Ames-Webster Mansion
9 Commonwealth Avenue
10 Burrage Mansion
11 J.P. Licks
12 Prudential Center Skywalk

Landfill projects executed between 1835 and 1882 created this area, which replaced a marshy body of water. The street pattern is a grid that contrasts with the crazy-quilt geography of the city's older neighborhoods. The streets here go in alphabetical order, starting at the Public Garden with Arlington Street and continuing across Massachusetts Avenue. This is mostly an outdoor excursion; in the heat of summer, try to get an early start. START: **Green Line to Arlington**

① ★★★ kids **Public Garden.** Today, Charles Street separates Boston Common from the Public Garden; in colonial times, it was the shore of the Charles River. On the night of April 18, 1775, British troops bound for Lexington and Concord boarded boats to Cambridge ("two if by sea") at the foot of the Common and set off across what's now the Public Garden. See p 15, bullet ⑥.

George Washington statue in the Public Garden.

② ★★ **George Washington statue.**
Boston's first equestrian statue guards the most dramatic entrance to the city's loveliest park. The 38-foot-tall (12m) statue is considered an excellent likeness of the first president, who was known as an outstanding horseman. The artist,

Thomas Ball, was a Charlestown native who worked in Italy. Among his students was noted sculptor Daniel Chester French (he created the Abraham Lincoln statue in Washington, D.C.'s Lincoln Memorial, among many other works). *Off Arlington St. at Commonwealth Ave.*

③ ★★★ **Commonwealth Avenue Mall.**
The centerpiece of architect Arthur Gilman's French-inspired design of the Back Bay is this dramatic boulevard, 240 feet (73m) wide with a 100-foot-wide (30m) mall down the center. Construction began in 1858, and by the late 1870s, the mall was important enough for landscape architect Frederick Law Olmsted to include it in his system of Boston parks known

The Commonwealth Avenue Mall.

as the Emerald Necklace. Beautiful buildings line both sides of Commonwealth Avenue, and a curious collection of statuary embellishes the mall; it begins with Alexander Hamilton (across Arlington St. from George Washington) and extends to Leif Eriksson (at the west end, not far from Kenmore Square). *Arlington St. to Charlesgate.*

④ ★ First Church in Boston.

The First Church in Boston is a direct successor to *the* first church in Boston. John Winthrop and his followers had barely landed in 1630 when they adopted the covenant that launched the congregation. This building dates to 1867, when the institution was known as the First and Second Church. The original architects, Ware and Van Brunt (who designed Harvard's Memorial Hall), intended the edifice to resemble an English country church. A fire in 1968 destroyed much of that building; Paul Rudolph's 1971 renovation preserves much of the remaining structure. Now Unitarian Universalist, the congregation voted to revert to the current name in 2005. ⏱: *15 min. 66 Marlborough St. (Berkeley St.).* ☎ *617/267-6730. www.fscboston.org. T: Green Line to Arlington.*

⑤ ★ First Baptist Church. The

legendary architect H. H. Richardson was just starting out when he designed this church, a Roxbury puddingstone structure with a 176-foot (54m) tower. This is the first church in the style now known as Richardsonian Romanesque (the best-known example is Trinity Church in nearby Copley Square). Completed in 1872, it originally belonged to the Brattle Square Unitarian Society, which sold it in 1882. It's notable not just for Richardson's work but for the contribution of another genius who soon went on to a considerably better-known project:

First Baptist Church. The trumpeters on the corners of this frieze are sometimes called "the bean blowers."

The frieze at the top of the tower is the work of Frédéric Auguste Bartholdi, designer of the Statue of Liberty. Louis Comfort Tiffany designed the stained-glass window depicting Jesus' baptism, but the three rose windows are the real treasures here. Almost every guidebook I've ever seen calls this building the "Church of the Holy Bean Blowers," but in more than 2 decades in Boston, I've never heard anyone call it that. ⏱: *15 min. 110 Commonwealth Ave. (Clarendon St.).* ☎ *617/267-3148. www.firstbaptist churchofboston.org. T: Green Line to Arlington.*

⑥ ★★ Vendome Memorial. On

June 17, 1972, fire devastated the former Hotel Vendome—and the Boston Fire Department. The fire in the lovely building at 160 Commonwealth Avenue had been extinguished and clean-up operations were under way when the southeast section of the structure unexpectedly collapsed. Nine firefighters were killed—the worst tragedy in the history of the department. The dramatic memorial, unveiled in 1997, is a low, curving black granite wall. The feature that pushes Ted Clausen's design from dramatic to heartbreaking is the bronze rendering of a firefighter's helmet atop a firefighter's coat draped over the wall. *Commonwealth Ave. at Dartmouth St.*

7 ★★ **Marlborough Street.** In contrast to the grandeur of Commonwealth Avenue, the commerce of Newbury Street, and the traffic of Beacon Street, Marlborough Street is a gracious residential thoroughfare. I'm sending you on a somewhat meandering route that includes a 2-block stretch of Marlborough Street to ensure that you appreciate the contrast. If you like what you see, take some extra time to go farther. *Clarendon St. to Exeter St.*

8 ★ **Ames-Webster Mansion.** Constructed in 1872 and enlarged in 1882, this Victorian landmark boasts some of the most elaborate exterior decoration in the Back Bay—and that's saying something. The building now holds offices; you can probably slip into the lobby and check out the interior ornamentation. *306 Dartmouth St. (Commonwealth Ave.). T: Green Line to Copley.*

9 ★★★ **Commonwealth Avenue.** The buildings that line "Comm. Ave." proceed in roughly chronological order. As the landfill

The Vendome Memorial.

that created the Back Bay neighborhood marched west, architectural styles grew wilder, leaving behind a few stretches where it hardly seems possible that the building facades could hold more ornamentation. Take your time as you explore this 4-block stretch, which abounds with gables, archways, medallions, fanciful wrought iron, and ornamental brickwork. *Dartmouth St. to Hereford St.*

10 **Burrage Mansion.** Inspired by the Château de Chenonceau in France's Loire Valley, the 1889 mansion designed by Charles Brigham is a rare Boston example of over-the-top French Renaissance architecture. The roof of the limestone building, now an assisted-living community, is especially ornate—check out the turrets. *314 Commonwealth Ave. (Hereford St.)*

11 ★★ **J. P. Licks.** A homegrown chain that specializes in superb gourmet ice cream, J. P. Licks gets its initials from the Jamaica Plain neighborhood—and an A-plus from aficionados. *352 Newbury St. (Hereford St. and Massachusetts Ave.)* ☎ *617/236-1666. $.*

Take some time to wander along lovely Marlborough Street.

⑫ ★★ **Prudential Center Skywalk.** Having seen the Back Bay from street level, you'll get a whole new perspective when you study it from above. The Skywalk, on the 50th floor of the Prudential Tower, affords views of far more than just the Back Bay—the 360-degree panorama extends as far as New Hampshire and Cape Cod when the sky is clear. Interactive audiovisual displays, including exhibits from the city's now-defunct immigration museum, trace Boston's history. 🕐: *1 hr. 800 Boylston St. (Fairfield St.) ☎ 617/859-0648. Daily 10am–10pm; always call first, because the space sometimes closes for private events. Admission $10.50 adults, $8.50 seniors, $7 kids under 12. Adults must show a photo ID to enter the Prudential Tower. T: Green Line E to Prudential, or B, C, or D to Hynes/ICA.* ●

Antiques

Shopping Best Bets

Best **Discount Shopping**
★★★ Filene's Basement,
426 Washington St. (p 82)

Most **Fun Gifts**
★★★ Joie de Vivre, *1792 Massachusetts Ave., Cambridge (p 85)*

Most **Socially Conscious Gifts**
★★★ Ten Thousand Villages, *694 Massachusetts Ave., Cambridge (p 86)*

Best **Sweet Spot**
★★ Dairy Fresh Candies, *57 Salem St. (p 84)*

Best **Costume Jewelry**
★★ High Gear Jewelry, *204 Hanover St. (p 86)*

Best **Fancy Jewelry**
★★ John Lewis, Inc., *97 Newbury St. (p 86)*

Best **Antiques**
★★★ Upstairs Downstairs Antiques, *93 Charles St. (p 78)*

Best **Children's Clothing**
★★ Calliope, *33 Brattle St., Cambridge (p 81)*

Best **Craft Supplies**
★★ Paper Source, *338 Boylston St. and branches (p 81)*

Best **Wedding Presents**
★★ Fresh Eggs, *58 Clarendon St. (p 85)*

Best **Home Decor**
★ Koo de Kir, *65 Chestnut St. (p 85)*

Best **Reason to Visit Harvard Square**
★★ Colonial Drug, *49 Brattle St., Cambridge (p 88)*

Best **Bubbles**
★★★ Lush, *166 Newbury St. (p 88)*

Best **Stationery**
★ Cross, *Zero Brattle St., Cambridge (p 85)*

Most **Teen-Friendly**
★ Newbury Comics, *332 Newbury St. and branches (p 88)*

Best **Salute to Texas**
★ Helen's Leather Shop, *110 Charles St. (p 84)*

Most **Parisian**
Diptyque, *123 Newbury St. (p 85)*

Harvard Square.

Downtown Boston Shopping

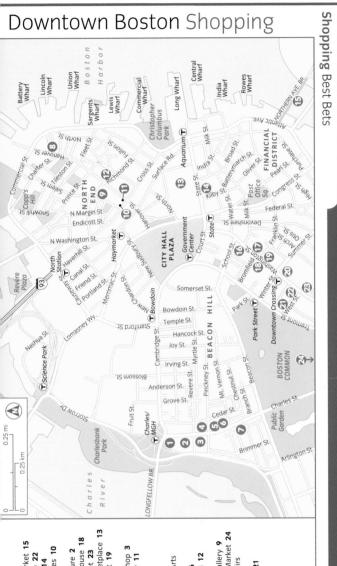

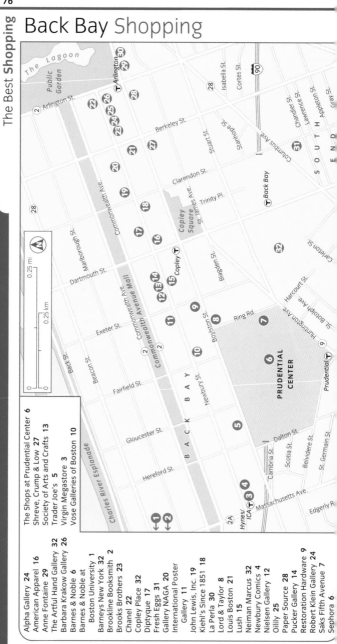

Harvard Square Shopping

Cambridge Shopping

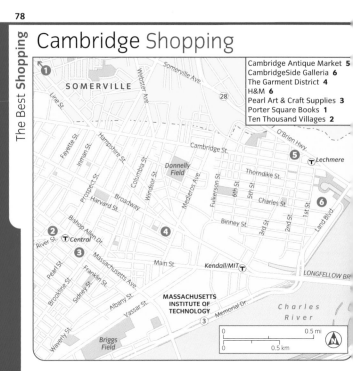

Cambridge Antique Market **5**
CambridgeSide Galleria **6**
The Garment District **4**
H&M **6**
Pearl Art & Craft Supplies **3**
Porter Square Books **1**
Ten Thousand Villages **2**

Boston Shopping **A to Z**

Antiques & Collectibles
★ **Danish Country Antique Furniture** BEACON HILL   The specialty here is Scandinavian furnishings from the 18th century to the present. *138 Charles St. (Revere St.).* ☎ *617/227-1804. AE, MC, V. T: Red Line to Charles/MGH. Map p 75.*

★★**Cambridge Antique Market** CAMBRIDGE   Five floors and some 150 dealers mean this is a hit-or-miss experience—with more hits than misses. Many of the merchants accept credit cards. *201 Msgr. O'Brien Hwy. (Third St.).* ☎ *617/868-9655. www.marketantique.com. T: Green Line to Lechmere. Map above.*

★★★ **Upstairs Downstairs Antiques** BEACON HILL

Arranged as a series of tastefully appointed rooms, the merchandise at this subterranean shop reflects a discerning eye and a nose for value. *93 Charles St. (Pinckney St.).* ☎ *617/367-1950. MC, V. T: Red Line to Charles/MGH. Map p 75.*

Art
★ **Alpha Gallery** BACK BAY
Contemporary American paintings, sculpture, and works on paper are the focus. *38 Newbury St., 7th floor (Berkeley St.).* ☎ *617/536-4465. www.alphagallery.com. MC, V. T: Green Line to Arlington. Map p 76.*

★ **Barbara Krakow Gallery**
BACK BAY   This long-standing gallery is an important destination

for post-1945 paintings, sculptures, drawings, and prints. *10 Newbury St., 5th floor (Arlington St.).* ☎ 617/262-4490. *www.barbarakrakow gallery.com. No credit cards. T: Green Line to Arlington. Map p 76.*

★★ **Gallery NAGA** BACK BAY This gallery inside the Church of the Covenant specializes in holography, photography, contemporary paintings, and studio furniture. *67 Newbury St. (Berkeley St.).* ☎ 617/267-9060. *www.gallerynaga.com. AE. T: Green Line to Arlington. Map p 76.*

★★★ **International Poster Gallery** BACK BAY The huge stock of French, Swiss, Italian, Soviet, and other international vintage posters here is always worth a look. *205 Newbury St. (Exeter and Fairfield sts.).* ☎ 617/375-0076. *www.internationalposter.com. AE, MC, V. T: Green Line to Copley. Map p 76.*

★★ **Nielsen Gallery** BACK BAY Nina Nielsen founded her gallery in 1963 and personally selects the contemporary artists who show here. *179 Newbury St. (Dartmouth and Exeter sts.).* ☎ 617/266-4835. *www. nielsengallery.com. AE, MC, V. T: Green Line to Copley. Map p 76.*

★★ **Pucker Gallery** BACK BAY Five floors of gallery space

encompass African, Asian, Israeli, and Inuit work, an impressive variety of contemporary art, photographs, and more. *171 Newbury St. (Dartmouth and Exeter sts.).* ☎ 617/267-9473. *www.puckergallery.com. MC, V. T: Green Line to Copley. Map p 76.*

★ **Robert Klein Gallery** BACK BAY This prestigious gallery represents fine-art photographers from the 19th through the 21st century. *38 Newbury St. (Arlington St.).* ☎ 617/267-7997. *www.robertklein gallery.com. AE, MC, V. T: Green Line to Arlington. Map p 76.*

★ **Vose Galleries of Boston** BACK BAY The specialty here is American paintings from the 18th through the early 20th century. *238 Newbury St. (Fairfield St.).* ☎ 617/536-3176. *www.vosegalleries.com. AE, MC, V. T: Green Line to Copley or Green Line B, C, or D to Hynes/ICA. Map p 76.*

Books
★ **kids Barnes & Noble** BACK BAY This branch of the national chain is almost always busy; check ahead for kids' events, especially on weekends. There's also a Barnes & Noble at Boston University. *Shops at Prudential Center, 800 Boylston St. (Fairfield St.).* ☎ 617/247-6959.

The International Poster Gallery.

www.bn.com. AE, DISC, MC, V. T: Green Line E to Prudential. Map p 76. Boston University store: 660 Beacon St. (Commonwealth Ave. and Deerfield St.). ☎ 617/267-8484. www. bu.bkstore.com. T: Green Line B, C, or D to Kenmore. Map p 76.

★ kids **Borders** DOWNTOWN CROSSING A huge store with three levels of books, music, magazines, and more. Author appearances are often scheduled here. The Cambridge branch is a smallish but welcome retreat in a busy mall. 10–24 School St. (Washington St.). ☎ 617/557-7188. www.bordersstores.com. AE, DISC, MC, V. T: Blue or Orange Line to State. Map p 75. Cambridge store: CambridgeSide Galleria, 100 CambridgeSide Place (First St. and Land Blvd.). ☎ 617/679-0887. T: Green Line to Lechmere. Map p 78.

★★ **Brattle Book Shop** DOWN-TOWN CROSSING One of the best used-book dealers around, the Brattle Book Shop also sells rare and out-of-print titles. 9 West St. (Washington and Tremont sts.). ☎ 800/447-9595. www.brattlebookshop. com. AE, MC, V. T: Red or Orange Line to Downtown Crossing. Map p 75.

★★★ kids **Brookline Book-smith** COOLIDGE CORNER An enormous selection and enthusiastic staff make this one of the Boston area's best bookstores. 279 Harvard St. (Beacon St.), Brookline. ☎ 617/566-6660. www.brooklinebooksmith. com. AE, DISC, MC, V. T: Green Line C to Coolidge Corner. Map p 76.

★ kids **Curious George Goes to WordsWorth** CAMBRIDGE A well-versed staff presides over Curious George's nearly encyclopedic stock of children's books. 1 John F. Kennedy St. (Brattle St.). ☎ 617/498-0062. www.curiousg.com. AE, DISC, MC, V. T: Red Line to Harvard. Map p 77.

★ **Globe Corner Bookstore** CAMBRIDGE The travel books, maps, atlases, and more at this recently relocated Harvard Square favorite will inspire you to wander. 90 Mount Auburn St. (John F. Kennedy St.). ☎ 800/358-6013. www.globe corner.com. AE, DISC, MC, V. T: Red Line to Harvard. Map p 77.

★★ **Harvard Book Store** CAM-BRIDGE Great selections of new books upstairs, remainders and used books downstairs, and bookworms everywhere. 1256 Massachusetts Ave. (Plympton St.). ☎ 800/542-323. www.harvard.com. AE, DISC, MC, V. T: Red Line to Harvard. Map p 77.

There are plenty of bargains to be found at Brattle Book Shop.

The Harvard Coop, a Harvard Square mainstay.

★ **The Harvard Coop** CAMBRIDGE   At the heart of Harvard Square is this excellent bookstore and logo-merchandise shop. It is *not* true that everyone looks smarter in a Harvard T-shirt. *1400 Massachusetts Ave. (Brattle St.).* ☎ *617/499-2000. www.thecoop.com. AE, MC, V. T: Red Line to Harvard. Map p 77.*

★ **kids** **Porter Square Books** CAMBRIDGE   This is a classic independent neighborhood bookstore—in a super-literate neighborhood. *Porter Square Shopping Center, 25 White St. (off Massachusetts Ave.).* ☎ *617/491-2220. www.porter squarebooks.com. AE, DISC, MC, V. T: Red Line to Porter. Map p 78.*

★ **Schoenhof's Foreign Books** CAMBRIDGE   If it's printed, bound, and in a language other than English, Schoenhof's likely stocks it or can order it. *76A Mount Auburn St. (Holyoke St.).* ☎ *617/547-8855. www.schoenhofs.com. AE, MC, V. T: Red Line to Harvard. Map p 77.*

Children: Fashion & Toys

★★ **kids** **Calliope** CAMBRIDGE   The clothing, shoes, toys, and gifts at this little shop are unusual enough to be special but not weird (a delicate balance). *33 Brattle St. (Brattle Sq.).* ☎ *617/876-4149. MC, V. T: Red Line to Harvard. Map p 77.*

kids **Oilily** BACK BAY   The Dutch brand is known internationally for its brightly colored, top-quality—with prices to match—children's and women's fashions. *32 Newbury St. (Arlington and Berkeley sts.).* ☎ *617/247-2386. www.oililyusa. com. AE, DISC, MC, V. T: Green Line to Arlington. Map p 76.*

★ **kids** **The Red Wagon** BEACON HILL   This welcoming space overflows with toys and gorgeous, pricey clothing and shoes for infants to preteens. *69 Charles St. (Mount Vernon St.).* ☎ *617/523-9402. AE, DISC, MC, V. T: Red Line to Charles/MGH. Map p 75.*

Craft Galleries & Craft Supplies

★ **The Artful Hand Gallery** BACK BAY   The handcrafted art at this delightful gallery includes jewelry, blown glass, ceramics, folk art, wood bowls and boxes, and furniture. *Copley Place, 100 Huntington Ave. (Dartmouth St.).* ☎ *617/262-9601. AE, DISC, MC, V. T: Orange Line to Back Bay. Map p 76.*

★★ **Paper Source** BACK BAY   Gorgeous wrapping, writing, and craft papers are the backdrop for an extensive selection of gifts, books, pens, stickers, stamps, and more. *338 Boylston St. (Arlington St.).* ☎ *617/536-3444. www.papersource.com. AE, DISC, MC, V. T: Green Line to Arlington. Map p 76.*

★ **Pearl Art & Craft Supplies** CAMBRIDGE   The two-level store carries paint, pencils, easels, envelopes, clay, canvas and more. *579 Massachusetts Ave. (Essex and Norfolk sts.).* ☎ *617/547-6600. www. pearlpaint.com. AE, DISC, MC, V. T: Red Line to Central. Map p 78.*

Filene's Basement has long been a favorite stop for bargain hunters.

★★ **Society of Arts and Crafts**
BACK BAY   This nonprofit society
specializes in contemporary American work. Items for sale are downstairs; the gallery is on the second
floor. *175 Newbury St. (Dartmouth
and Exeter sts.).* ☎ *617/266-1810.
www.societyofcrafts.org. AE, MC, V.
T: Green Line to Copley. Map p 76.*

★ **Windsor Button** DOWNTOWN
CROSSING   Buttons—nice. Sewing
notions—excellent. Everything you'd
ever need for knitting and crochet-
ing—hold me back. *35 Temple Place
(Washington and Tremont sts.).*
☎ *617/482-4969. www.windsor
button.com. AE, MC, V. T: Red or
Orange Line to Downtown Crossing.
Map p 75.*

Department Stores
★★ **Lord & Taylor** BACK BAY
An excellent destination for
women's special-occasion finery.
Lord & Taylor also has terrific men's
and cosmetics departments and
great sales. *760 Boylston St. (Exeter
St.).* ☎ *617/262-6000. www.lordand
taylor.com. AE, DISC, MC, V. T: Green
Line to Copley. Map p 76.*

Macy's DOWNTOWN CROSSING
The anchor store of Downtown
Crossing, Macy's carries a wide
selection of fashion, cosmetics,
housewares, china, and silver.
450 Washington St. (Summer St.).
☎ *617/357-3000. www.macys.com.*

*AE, MC, V. T: Red or Orange Line to
Downtown Crossing. Map p 75.*

★ **Neiman Marcus** BACK BAY
When you're shopping for the person
who has everything and money is no
object, this is the place. *5 Copley
Place, 100 Huntington Ave. (Dartmouth St.).* ☎ *617/536-3660. www.
neimanmarcus.com. AE, DISC, MC,
V. T: Orange Line to Back Bay. Map
p 76.*

Saks Fifth Avenue BACK BAY
Fashion, cosmetics, and shoes
galore make Saks one of the New
York names Bostonians have
embraced without any complaints.
*Prudential Plaza, 786 Boylston St.
(Ring Rd.).* ☎ *617/262-8500. www.
saksfifthavenue.com. AE, DISC, MC,
V. T: Green Line to Prudential. Map
p 76.*

Discount Shopping
★★★ **Filene's Basement** DOWN-
TOWN CROSSING   The original.
Prices drop automatically after mer-
chandise is on sale for 2 weeks.
Look for designer duds in the Vault.
*426 Washington St. (Summer and
Franklin sts.).* ☎ *617/348-7848.
www.filenesbasement.com. AE,
DISC, MC, V. T: Red or Orange Line to
Downtown Crossing. Map p 75.*

★ **DSW Shoe Warehouse**
DOWNTOWN CROSSING   Dis-
counted men's and women's shoes
cram two floors. The real bargains

are on the clearance racks. *385 Washington St. (Bromfield St.).* ☎ *617/556-0052. www.dswshoe. com. AE, DISC, MC, V. T: Red or Orange Line to Downtown Crossing. Map p 75.*

★ **Eddie Bauer Outlet** DOWNTOWN CROSSING   The sportswear specialist nicks some prices and slashes others at this large, well-maintained store. *500 Washington St. (Temple Place).* ☎ *617/423-4722. www.eddiebaueroutlet.com. AE, DISC, MC, V. T: Red or Orange Line to Downtown Crossing. Map p 75.*

Fashion

★ **American Apparel** BACK BAY   The anti-sweatshop pioneer creates fun T-shirts, sexy tanks, and other comfy knits—and makes them in downtown Los Angeles. *138 Newbury St. (Dartmouth St.).* ☎ *617/ 536-4768. www.americanapparel. net. AE, DISC, MC, V. T: Green Line to Copley. Map p 76.*

★ **Anne Fontaine** BACK BAY   This French designer's specialty is perfect white blouses. Pastels sometimes sneak in (and once I saw black!), but it's really all about the white blouses. *318 Boylston St. (Arlington St.).* ☎ *617/423-0366.*

www.annefontaine.com. AE, MC, V. T: Green Line to Arlington. Map p 76.

★★ **Barneys New York** BACK BAY   The New York–based luxury store specializes in men's and women's designer fashions and cosmetics. And the women's shoe department is gigantic. *Copley Place, 100 Huntington Ave. (Dartmouth St.).* ☎ *617/385-3300. www.barneys. com. AE, MC, V. T: Orange Line to Back Bay. Map p 76.*

★ **Berk's Shoes** CAMBRIDGE   A Harvard Square standby, Berk's stocks the latest trends in footwear plus classic lines from Birkenstock to Converse. *50 John F. Kennedy St. (Winthrop St.).* ☎ *888/462-3757. www.berkshoes.com. AE, DISC, MC, V. T: Red Line to Harvard. Map p 77.*

★ **Brooks Brothers** BACK BAY   A mainstay of traditional New England "fashion." The lawyers and bankers shop at the financial district branch downtown. *46 Newbury St. (Berkeley St.).* ☎ *617/267-2600. www.brooksbrothers.com. AE, DISC, MC, V. T: Green Line to Arlington. Map p 76. Financial district store: 75 State St. (Kilby and Broad sts.).* ☎ *617/261-9990. T: Blue or Orange Line to State. Map p 75.*

Take a break from gallery-hopping on Newbury Street to shop for designer duds at Brooks Brothers or Chanel.

★★ **Chanel** BACK BAY   The Ritz-Carlton, Boston, is home to the French fashion legend's only free-standing Boston boutique. *5 Newbury St. (Arlington St.).* ☎ *617/859-0055. www.chanel.com. AE, MC, V. T: Green Line to Arlington. Map p 76.*

★ **The Garment District** CAMBRIDGE   Fantastic deals on vintage clothing and accessories. First-floor merchandise costs $1.50 a pound. *200 Broadway (Davis St.).* ☎ *617/876-5230. www.garmentdistrict.com. AE, DISC, MC, V. T: Red Line to Kendall/MIT. Map p 78.*

★ **kids H&M** DOWNTOWN CROSSING   The cheap-chic fashion magnet carries the latest clothing and accessories for men, women, and kids at its Boston location. The Cambridge branch carries styles for women and teens of both sexes. *350 Washington St. (Franklin St.).* ☎ *617/482-7001. www.hm.com. AE, MC, V. T: Red or Orange Line to Downtown Crossing. Map p 75. Cambridge store: CambridgeSide Galleria, 100 CambridgeSide Place (First St. and Land Blvd.).* ☎ *617/225-0895. T: Green Line to Lechmere, or Red Line to Kendall/MIT and mall shuttle. Map p 78.*

★ **Helen's Leather Shop** BEACON HILL   Western boots and shirts, leather jackets and coats, and beautiful accessories make Helen's a particular favorite with displaced Texans. *110 Charles St. (Pinckney St.).* ☎ *617/742-2077. www.helensleather.com. AE, DISC, MC, V. T: Red Line to Charles/MGH. Map p 75.*

★ **Injeanius** NORTH END   Jeans by well-known and up-and-coming designers. Prices can be steep. *441 Hanover St. (Salutation and Battery sts.).* ☎ *617/523-5326. AE, MC, V. T: Green or Orange Line to Haymarket. Map p 75.*

★ **La Perla** BACK BAY   If my lingerie wardrobe contained these gorgeous Italian concoctions, I might never get dressed. And not just because I wouldn't be able to afford clothes. *250 Boylston St. (Arlington St.).* ☎ *617/423-5709. www.laperla.com. AE, MC, V. T: Green Line to Arlington. Map p 76.*

★ **Louis Boston** BACK BAY   Louis (say "Louie's") was chic Bostonians' automatic destination for men's and women's designer fashions long before Barneys New York hit town. *234 Berkeley St. (Newbury and Boylston sts.).* ☎ *800/225-5135. www.louisboston.com. AE, MC, V. T: Green Line to Arlington. Map p 76.*

★★ **Oona's** HARVARD SQUARE   Oona's carries a huge but choice stock of vintage clothing, accessories, and jewelry. *1210 Massachusetts Ave. (Arrow St.).* ☎ *617/491-2654. AE, MC, V. T: Red Line to Harvard. Map p 77.*

Food & Candy

★★ **Dairy Fresh Candies** NORTH END   All sorts of sweets share this tiny space with imported Italian specialties and much more. *57 Salem St. (Cross St.).* ☎ *800/336-5536. www.dairyfreshcandies.com. AE, MC, V. T: Green or Orange Line to Haymarket. Map p 75.*

Oona's celebrated its 30th anniversary in 2003.

★ **Salumeria Italiana** NORTH END The best Italian grocery store in town carries cheeses, meats, pastas, olive oils, vinegars, fresh bread, and more. Picnic, anyone? *151 Richmond St. (Hanover St.).* ☎ *800/400-5916. www.salumeriaitaliana.com. MC, V. T: Green or Orange Line to Haymarket. Map p 75.*

★ **Savenor's** BEACON HILL An excellent gourmet market with an intriguing specialty (exotic meat, like buffalo and rattlesnake), Savenor's is a perfect picnic launching pad. *160 Charles St. (Cambridge St.).* ☎ *617/723-6328. www.savenorsmarket.com. AE, MC, V. T: Red Line to Charles/MGH. Map p 75. Cambridge store: 92 Kirkland St.* ☎ *617/576-6328. T: Red Line to Harvard, 20-min. walk.*

★★★ **Trader Joe's** BACK BAY The California-based grocery-store chain specializes in natural and organic basics and treats, including prepared foods. *899 Boylston St. (Gloucester St.).* ☎ *617/262-6505. www.traderjoes.com. MC, V. T: Green Line B, C, or D to Hynes/ICA. Map p 76.*

Gifts & Home Accessories

★ **Abodeon** CAMBRIDGE The vintage and retro home and kitchen accessories and furnishings here date from the mid–20th century—or look as if they do. *1731 Massachusetts Ave. (Garfield and Prentiss sts.).* ☎ *617/497-0137. AE, MC, V. T: Red Line to Porter. Map p 77.*

★★ kids **Black Ink** BEACON HILL The constantly changing stock of funky gifts and household items, games, toys, and office accessories means Black Ink is never the same twice. The Harvard Square branch is equally delightful. *101 Charles St. (Revere and Pinckney sts).* ☎ *617/723-3883. AE, DC, MC, V. T: Red Line to Charles/MGH. Map p 75. Cambridge store: 5 Brattle St. (John F.*

Kennedy St.). ☎ *617/497-1221. T: Red Line to Harvard. Map p 77.*

★ **Cross** CAMBRIDGE Yes, the pen company. You'll need a nice pen to suit the gorgeous stationery and cards at this tiny Harvard Square shop. *Zero Brattle St. (Palmer St.).* ☎ *617/868-7020. www.cross.com. AE, DISC, MC, V. T: Red Line to Harvard. Map p 77.*

★ **Diptyque** BACK BAY The beloved Parisian candles are the centerpiece of this little shop, one of Diptyque's two North American locations (the other is in San Francisco). *123 Newbury St. (Clarendon and Dartmouth sts.).* ☎ *617/351-2430. www.diptyqueusa.com. AE, MC, V. T: Green Line to Copley. Map p 76.*

★★ **Fresh Eggs** SOUTH END Fresh, funky home accessories, from furniture to napkins and tablecloths, plus kitchen equipment and why-didn't-I-think-of-that gadgets. *58 Clarendon St. (Chandler St.).* ☎ *617/247-8150. AE, MC, V. T: Orange Line to Back Bay. Map p 76.*

★★★ **Joie de Vivre** CAMBRIDGE My favorite gift shop carries an incredible selection of sophisticated and retro toys, jewelry, note cards, puzzles, and novelty items. *1792 Massachusetts Ave. (Arlington St.).* ☎ *617/864-8188. AE, MC, V. T: Red Line to Porter. Map p 77.*

★ **Koo de Kir** BEACON HILL Contemporary style on Beacon Hill is unexpected but delightful—like the well-edited selection of gifts, jewelry, furniture, and home and kitchen accessories here. *65 Chestnut St. (Charles St.).* ☎ *617/723-8111. www.koodekir.com. AE, MC, V. T: Red Line to Charles/MGH. Map p 75.*

★ **Museum of Fine Arts Gift Shop** FANEUIL HALL MARKETPLACE The merchandise here is a "greatest hits" selection of items from the museum's in-house shop.

3 South Market Building (Chatham Row). ☎ 617/720-1266. www.mfa shop.org. AE, DISC, MC, V. T: Green or Blue Line to Government Center. Map p 75.

★ kids Restoration Hardware

BACK BAY   Fun home accessories, retro toys and gifts, furniture, and, of course, hardware make this branch of the chain terrific for browsing. *711 Boylston St. (Exeter St.).* ☎ *617/578-0088. www.restorationhardware. com. AE, MC, V. T: Green Line to Copley. Map p 76.*

★ Shake the Tree Gallery

NORTH END   More boutique than gallery, Shake the Tree carries gorgeous jewelry, crafts, clothing, home accessories, candles, ceramics, and the like. *95 Salem St. (Cross and Parmenter sts.).* ☎ *617/742-0484. MC, V. T: Green or Orange Line to Haymarket. Map p 75.*

★ kids Ten Thousand Villages

CENTRAL SQUARE   The fair-trade chain specializes in handicrafts—folk art, home accessories, and more—by international artisans. *694 Massachusetts Ave. (Western Ave. and Pleasant St.).* ☎ *617/876-*

2414. www.tenthousandvillages. com. DISC, MC, V. T: Red Line to Central. Map p 78.

★ kids The Games People Play

CAMBRIDGE   Come here for board games, puzzles, chess and backgammon sets, and anything else you need to turn a coffee table into a playground. *1100 Massachusetts Ave. (Mount Auburn St.).* ☎ *800/696-0711. AE, DISC, MC, V. T: Red Line to Harvard. Map p 77.*

Jewelry

★★ High Gear Jewelry NORTH

END   Classic and contemporary costume jewelry beckons from the front window of this shop on the Freedom Trail. *204 Hanover St. (Cross St.).* ☎ *617/523-5084. MC, V. T: Green or Orange Line to Haymarket. Map p 75.*

★★★ John Lewis, Inc. BACK BAY

Unique designs crafted on the premises in platinum, gold, and silver are both lovely and imaginative. *97 Newbury St. (Clarendon St.).* ☎ *617/266-6665. www.johnlewisinc.com. MC, V. T: Green Line to Arlington. Map p 76.*

If you can't afford the real thing, shop for prints, art books, and more at the Museum of Fine Arts Gift Shop.

Faneuil Hall Marketplace.

★ **Shreve, Crump & Low** BACK BAY Boston's answer to Tiffany's features fine jewelry as well as unique items like gurgling cod pitchers. *440 Boylston St. (Berkeley St.).* ☎ *617/267-9100. www.shrevecrumpandlow.com. AE, MC, V. T: Green Line to Arlington. Map p 76.*

Malls & Shopping Centers
kids CambridgeSide Galleria CAMBRIDGE The mall at home probably has one of every store here. Kids may enjoy that comfort level. *100 CambridgeSide Place (Land Blvd. and First St.).* ☎ *617/ 621-8666. www.shopcambridgeside. com. T: Green Line to Lechmere, or Red Line to Kendall/MIT and mall shuttle. Map p 78.*

★★ **Copley Place** BACK BAY This is a bustling enclave of boutiques and high-end mall brands, plus an occasional local merchant. It adjoins the Shops at Prudential Center (see below). *100 Huntington Ave. (Dartmouth St.).* ☎ *617/369-5000. www.shopcopleyplace.com. T: Orange Line to Back Bay. Map p 76.*

★ **kids Faneuil Hall Marketplace** DOWNTOWN Somewhat generic retail doesn't keep shoppers from flocking to the five-building marketplace. Check the pushcarts for more creative items. *North, Congress, and State sts. and Atlantic Ave.* ☎ *617/338-2323. www.faneuilhall marketplace.com. T: Green or Blue Line to Government Center. Map p 75.*

★ **kids The Shops at Prudential Center** BACK BAY "The Pru" mixes mostly unsurprising shops and boutiques with pushcarts holding crafts and novelty items. *800 Boylston St. (Fairfield St.).* ☎ *800/746-7778. www. prudentialcenter.com. T: Green Line E to Prudential or Green Line to Copley. Map p 76.*

Markets
★★ **Boston Public Market** WATERFRONT Produce, flowers, artisan cheeses, breads, and more are for sale on a pedestrian-only bridge. Open July to November Monday and Thursday from 11:30am to 7pm. *Northern Avenue Bridge (Atlantic Ave.).* ☎ *617/263-3355. www.bostonpublicmarket.org. No credit cards. T: Blue Line to Aquarium. Map p 75.*

★ **kids South End Open Market** SOUTH END This funky market offers art, crafts, produce, flowers, and baked goods. Open Sundays late May through October from 10am to 5pm. *540 Harrison Ave. (Randolph St.).* ☎ *617/481-2257.*

www.southendopenmarket.com. No credit cards. T: Orange Line to Back Bay, 10-min walk. Map p 75.

Music

★ Newbury Comics BACK BAY New and used CDs, including imports and independent labels, are the big draw, but check out the novelty items, T-shirts, posters, and comics. The original location is the best. *332 Newbury St. (Hereford St. and Massachusetts Ave.).* ☎ *617/ 236-4930. www.newbury.com. AE, DISC, MC, V. T: Green Line B, C, or D to Hynes/ICA. Map p 76.*

★★ Twisted Village CAMBRIDGE Free jazz, psychedelic rock, collectible reissues, the store's own label— I'm overwhelmed! How a place this funky snuck into chain-saturated Harvard Square is a puzzle. *12B Eliot St. (Bennett St.)* ☎ *617/354-6896. www.twistedvillage.com. MC, V. T: Red Line to Harvard. Map p 77.*

★ kids Virgin Megastore BACK BAY Three stories of music, plasma TVs, interactive kiosks, and other distractions make this store a magnet for kids of all ages. *360 Newbury St. (Massachusetts Ave.).* ☎ *617/896-0950. www.virginmega magazine.com. AE, DISC, MC, V. T: Green Line B, C, or D to Hynes/ICA. Map p 76.*

Perfume & Cosmetics

★★ Colonial Drug HARVARD SQUARE My favorite perfume— so obscure that department stores haven't stocked it in years—is one of the 1,000 fragrances here (along with numerous body-care products). *49 Brattle St. (Church St. and Appian Way).* ☎ *617/864-2222. No credit cards. T: Red Line to Harvard. Map p 77.*

★ Kiehl's Since 1851 BACK BAY The skin, hair, and body preparations here have a (deservedly) cult-like following. *112 Newbury St. (Clarendon St.).* ☎ *617/247-1777. www.kiehls.com. AE, DC, MC, V. T: Green Line to Copley. Map p 76.*

★★★ Lush BACK BAY The U.K.–based chain is known for fresh, organic, and natural products— including solid shampoo and "bath bombs"—that smell fantastic. *166 Newbury St. (Dartmouth and Exeter sts.).* ☎ *617/375-5874. www.lush. com. No credit cards. T: Green Line to Copley. Map p 76.*

★ Sephora BACK BAY This large self-service boutique carries a vast assortment of cosmetics and fragrances, with plenty of testers and a helpful staff. *Shops at Prudential Center, 800 Boylston St. (Fairfield St.).* ☎ *617/262-4200. www. sephora.com. AE, DISC, MC, V. T: Green Line to Copley. Map p 76.* ●

Sephora's large selection and ample supply of testers make it easy to browse for your new favorite fragrance.

5

The Best of the
Outdoors

The Public Garden & Boston Common

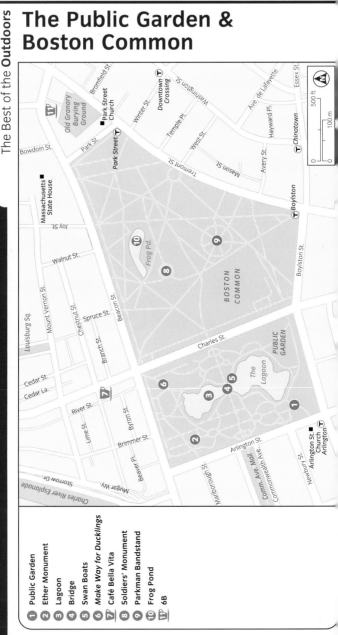

When asked to explain the difference between the Public Garden and the Common, I usually go for the easy analogy. The Public Garden is Boston's front yard, where everyone can see how beautiful this year's flowers are; Boston Common is the backyard, where the kids play ball and that one dusty patch just won't go away. START: **Green Line to Arlington**

1 ★★★ **kids** **Public Garden.** The 19th century left an indelible mark on Boston, and nowhere is that mark more permanent or more pleasant than in the Public Garden. The city set aside this land in the 1820s, the institution was formally established in 1837, and creating the nation's first public botanical garden out of a marshy riverbank and a lot of landfill took over 2 decades. By the late 1850s, the Public Garden had assumed roughly the form you see today—but there's nothing rough about it. These 24 acres (10ha) crisscrossed with walkways hold hundreds of formally arranged trees and shrubs, five fountains, and dozens of statues and memorials (the gardens of Versailles inspired the original plan). The exquisite flower beds change regularly, complementing the perennial plantings and giving the staid design a dynamic component. Besides walking and resting, the actual activities here aren't much—other than taking a ride on a Swan Boat, or tossing a snack to a duck. Let the low-tech atmosphere set the pace for you, though, and before long you'll realize that you can't remember why you were feeling so hyper when you arrived. Was that really half an hour ago? We just sat down for a minute. . . . *See p 15, bullet* **6**.

2 ★ **Ether Monument.** The oldest statue in the Public Garden, erected in 1868, celebrates the first use of general anesthesia in an operation. The procedure, the removal of a jaw tumor, took place at Massachusetts General Hospital in 1846, and

the monument was commissioned a mere 20 years later. In Boston, a city that does nothing quickly, this was clearly a big deal. The sculpture atop the monument—an elaborate confection, in keeping with the fashion of the time—is John Quincy Adams Ward's depiction of the Good Samaritan. The pool at the base represents healing, but the streams of water that once issued from the lions' heads (I did say it was elaborate) no longer function. A drive is under way to restore the former glory of the deteriorated monument.

3 ★★ **Lagoon.** The 3-acre (1ha) lagoon is a triumph of optical illusion—viewed from above, it's tiny, but from anywhere along the curving shore, it looks huge. With the completion of the signature water feature in 1861, George F. Meacham's design of the Public Garden was substantially complete. Today it's home to the Swan Boats

Ether Monument.

(see below), two pairs of live swans (Romeo, Juliet, Castor, and Pollux), and numerous ducks, who nest on the islands. Designed to resemble an English pond, the lagoon is temptingly cool in the heat of summer, but I strongly suggest that you play by the rules and stay out—I've seen the basin drained, and it's not pretty.

4 ★★ **Bridge.** The word "adorable" has no place in a discussion of landscape architecture, but this thing is seriously cute. It sits at the heart of the Public Garden, surrounded by colorful flower beds and swarming with pedestrians. Step away, perhaps to the shore of the lagoon, to appreciate the bridge's graceful proportions. An urban myth claims it's a copy of the Brooklyn Bridge, but they look nothing alike.

5 ★★ **kids** **Swan Boats.** In keeping with the Victorian atmosphere of the rest of the Public Garden, the main attraction is a fancy version of something simple. Each pedal-powered vessel (the employees do the pedaling) has an elaborate swan at the back, concealing the pedaling mechanism and transforming a humble boat ride into a reminder of a legendary opera. Robert Paget, who founded the Swan Boats in 1877, got the idea from the swan-drawn boat in the Wagner opera *Lohengrin*. Your

The Make Way for Ducklings *sculpture is a popular photo op for visitors with kids.*

family may associate it with *The Trumpet of the Swan,* a children's book by E. B. White, better known as the author of *Charlotte's Web* and *Stuart Little*. If you can't get to the Public Garden during Swan Boat hours, the dock is still worth a look—the boats tied up at night are one of the city's best photo ops. See p 23, bullet **6**.

6 ★★★ *Make Way for Ducklings.* Do you know the story of Mrs. Mallard and her eight babies, Jack, Kack, Lack, Mack, Nack, Ouack, Pack, and Quack? You will soon. Robert McCloskey's 1941 book introduces young readers to Boston, where the Mallard family goes in search of a new place to live.

The Public Garden's bridge is one of the smallest suspension bridges in the world.

After perilous adventures, they arrive at the Public Garden. The story was already beloved around the world when the three-dimensional version was conceived. Sculptor Nancy Schön's graceful rendering of McCloskey's charcoal drawings was unveiled in 1987, the 150th anniversary of the Public Garden. Her sculptures, created using the lost-wax process, capture the imagination of just about everyone who encounters the row of bronze waterfowl waddling in the direction of the water.

7 Café Bella Vita. Try to snag a window seat so you can take in the action on Beacon Hill's main street as you sip coffee and snack on gelato or a pastry. *30 Charles St. (Chestnut St.)* ☎ *617/720-4505. $.*

8 ★ Soldiers' Monument. Set aside as public land in 1634, Boston Common has been in constant use ever since—no wonder it looks so tired. Over the years, these 45 acres (18ha) have held pasture, barracks, gallows, a cemetery, parade grounds, ball fields, and more; today the Common sits atop a parking garage and two subway stations. Almost everywhere you look, you'll see plaques, statues, fountains, memorials, and monuments. The most prominent sits atop the highest point on the Common, Flagstaff Hill. The Soldiers' Monument, also known as the Soldiers' and Sailors' Monument, is the work of Martin Milmore, an Irish immigrant who apprenticed under Thomas Ball, the sculptor of the equestrian George Washington in the Public Garden (see p. 69, bullet **2**). Dedicated in 1877—when, it's worth remembering, the gold standard in public art was over-the-top ornate—it commemorates Boston residents who died in the Civil War.

9 ★ Parkman Bandstand. The Classical Revival bandstand, beautifully restored in the mid–1990s, sits at the center of a particularly lovely network of paths surrounded by stately trees. It's used for concerts and other events. The bandstand bears the name of George Francis Parkman, who died in 1908, leaving the city $5.5 million to be used for the maintenance of the Common.

10 ★★ Frog Pond. There's a logical explanation for this cute name: In Colonial times, frogs lived in the pond here. Today the Frog Pond is a skating rink in the winter, a wading pool in the summer, and a reflecting pool in the spring and fall. The location is serendipitous: Visitors enjoy an unusual perspective on the dome of the State House. *www.bostoncommonfrogpond.org.*

11 ★ 6B. The pleasant atmosphere and appetizer menu make this lounge a good place to unwind after exploring; time your visit so you arrive before the noisy afterwork crowd (the doors open at 11am). *6B Beacon St (Somerset St.)* ☎ *617/742-8565. $–$$.*

The Public Garden is particularly lovely when the flowers bloom in spring and summer.

The Esplanade

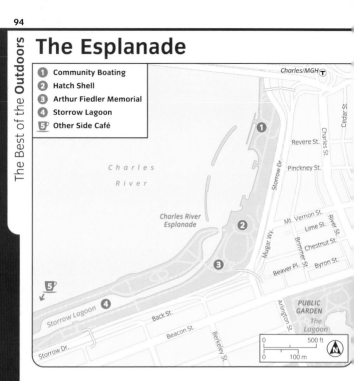

1 Community Boating
2 Hatch Shell
3 Arthur Fiedler Memorial
4 Storrow Lagoon
5 Other Side Café

Charles/MGH Ⓣ

Charles River

Charles River Esplanade

Storrow Lagoon

Back St.

Beacon St.

Storrow Dr.

Revere St.

Pinckney St.

Mt. Vernon St.

Lime St.

Chestnut St.

Beaver Pl. St.

Byron St.

Charles St.

Cedar St.

Storrow Dr.

Mugar Wy.

Brimmer St.

River St.

Arlington St.

Berkeley St.

PUBLIC GARDEN

The Lagoon

0   500 ft
0   100 m

Everyone has a place that they take for granted until out-of-towners start raving about it. For many Bostonians, the Esplanade is that place—it's where we meet friends to go walking (or running, biking, or skating) on the weekend or after work. We don't really think about it. Then someone reminds us that it's gorgeous and interesting, and we take another look. START: **Red Line to Charles/MGH. Cross the footbridge over Storrow Drive and turn left (keeping the river on your right).**

1 **Community Boating.** The first building you'll pass is this lovely boathouse. Community Boating moved here in 1941, but was first established in 1936 (it's the oldest public sailing program in the country). Thousands of people have learned to sail under its cooperative structure, initially designed to keep local youth off the streets of Depression-era Boston. To this day, kids 10 to 18 can sail all summer for just $1. It's a good deal for visitors, too—

$100 for two days of unlimited use in the Charles River basin. *21 David G. Mugar Way.* ☎ *617/523-1038.* *www.community-boating.org.*

2 ★★ **Hatch Shell.** The Charles River Esplanade evolved slowly into the pleasant park you see today, which rests on landfill. The river originally ended in a tidal basin rimmed with reeking mud flats; before the river was dammed in 1910. What's now the Charles River basin was an

The Community Boating fleet includes 13- to 23-foot (4m–7m) sailboats, kayaks, and windsurfers.

outrage to both eyes and noses (which is why the magnificent old residences on Beacon Street face the land, not the water). By 1929, the Esplanade was home to a temporary venue for the Boston Pops. Executing landscape architect Arthur Shurcliff's design of the Esplanade, which involved creating new land from fill pumped off the river bottom, took 5 unsightly years. The permanent Hatch Shell—formally the Edward Hatch Memorial Shell—was built in 1940 according to a graceful design by Richard Shaw. The amphitheater bears the names of 86 composers; look for your favorites, paying close attention to Sousa and Tchaikovsky, the stars of the Pops' annual Fourth of July concert. Stroll around the shell, an Art Deco confection with a rustic terrazzo exterior; if you arrive at the right time, you can plunk down on the lawn to listen to some music. Free events take over the stage almost every night in the summer, making this one of Boston's most popular cultural venues. *State Department of Conservation and Recreation: www.mass.gov/dcr/hatch_events.htm.*

3 ★★★ **The Arthur Fiedler Memorial.** Sculptor Ralph Helmick created this unforgettable memorial to the legendary conductor of the Boston Pops. Installed in 1985, it consists of stacked plates of sand-blasted aluminum that blend into an uncanny likeness of the head of Fiedler (1894–1979), who presided over the

Pops from 1930 until his death. To appreciate the full impact, note that, in Helmick's words, the sculpture "reads most coherently from afar"—a commentary on the contrast between Fiedler's public and private persona.

4 ★ **Storrow Lagoon.** An important feature of the Esplanade's design, the lagoon stretches more or less from Exeter Street to Fairfield Street (though the actual streets don't extend this far). I especially love the little bridges at either end of the narrow lagoon, which is surrounded by elaborate plantings and shady trees. The busy parkway to your left is Storrow Drive. Construction began in 1949, encroaching on the Esplanade. Rather than allow the parkland to shrink permanently, the state created islands offshore.

5 ★ **Other Side Café.** The closest Boston gets to California, this boho hangout is beloved for its veggie-friendly food and encyclopedic smoothie and juice menu. *407 Newbury St. (Massachusetts Ave.).* ☎ *617/536-9477. $–$$.*

The Arthur Fiedler Memorial.

Boston's **Colonial Cemeteries**

City Square
New Rutherford Ave
Chelsea St
CHARLESTOWN
Pier 4
CHARLESTOWN
NAVY YARD

Paul Revere Park
CHARLESTOWN BR.
Inner Harbor
Fiskes Wharf
Constitution Wharf

93
Revere Plaza
Langone Park
Commercial St
Battery Wharf
Lincoln Wharf

Nashua St
Sheafe St
Snow Hill St
Charter St
Tileston St
Hanover St
North St
Union Wharf

Lomasney Wy
North Station
Prince St
Endicott St
N Margin St
Salem St
NORTH END
Fleet St
Moon St
Lewis St
Sargents Wharf
Lewis Wharf

Causeway St
Canal St
Friend St
Portland St
Valenti Wy
Merrimac St
Haverhill St
N Washington St
Richmond St
North St
Fulton St
Commercial St
Commercial Wharf

New Chardon St
Bullfinch Pl
New Sudbury St
Hanover St
Cross St
Atlantic Ave
Christopher Columbus Park

Haymarket
5
3

Merrimac St
Congress St
North St
Surface Rd
Long Wharf

Staniford St
Bowdoin
CITY HALL PLAZA
Aquarium
Central Wharf

Cambridge St
New Chardon St
Bulfinch Pl
North St

Russell St
Joy St
Hancock St
Temple St
Bowdoin St
Somerset St
Government Center
State St
Central St
Milk St
India St
India Wharf

Myrtle St
Court St
State
Rowes Wharf

BEACON HILL
School St
Water St
Broad St

Beacon St
Park St
Bromfield St
1
2
Kilby St
Pearl St
Oliver St
High St

Park Street
Winter St
Milk St
Devonshire St
Post Office Square
FINANCIAL DISTRICT
NORTHERN AVE. BR. (pedestrian)

BOSTON COMMON
Downtown Crossing
Washington St
Franklin St
Federal St
Arch St
Congress St
EVELYN MOAKLEY BR.

Tremont St
Mason St
West St
Summer St
Otis St
Atlantic Ave

Boylston
Avery St
Ave. de Lafayette
Chauncy St
Kingston St
Lincoln St
Purchase St

Boylston St
Chinatown
Essex St
South Station

CHINATOWN
LaGrange
Beach St
South St
0   0.25 mi
0   0.25 km

Stuart St

1 **Old Granary Burying Ground**
2 **King's Chapel Burying Ground**
3 **Lulu's Bake Shoppe**
4 **Copp's Hill Burying Ground**
5 **Boston Beanstock Coffee Co.**

Colonial Boston was about **one-third the size** of the present-day city. Its residents clustered in what's now the downtown area, where they lived, worked, worshiped, and even buried their dead. The city was over 2 centuries old when Cambridge's Mount Auburn Cemetery (see p 63, bullet ⑧) opened in 1831, heralding the new custom of establishing cemeteries outside of population centers. START: **Red or Green Line to Park St.**

① ★★ **Old Granary Burying Ground.** Originally a section of Boston Common, this burying ground was laid out in 1660. It got its name from the granary, or grain-storage building, that once stood on the site of Park Street Church. Solomon Willard, architect of the Bunker Hill Monument, designed the granite entrance. Wander the walkways, learn a bit about the regular people buried here, and take in the diversity of markers and ornamental carvings. When the King's Chapel and Burying Ground (see below) was established, life in the New World was daunting, and the skulls, bones, and scary animals that dominate its headstone decorations reflect that. By the time this graveyard opened, life was more stable, and the afterlife apparently felt a bit less intimidating. Here you'll see the graves of

Paul Revere's grave, Old Granary Burying Ground.

Paul Revere, Samuel Adams, Peter Faneuil (who donated Faneuil Hall to Boston; his monument says "FUNAL"), the victims of the Boston Massacre, Benjamin Franklin's parents, and the wife of Isaac Vergoose—also known as Elizabeth Foster Goose; she's believed to be "Mother Goose." Even in death, John Hancock has a little more style than everyone else: The carving on his monument is a rebus. Look for the hand above the three birds, or cocks; "hand-cocks," get it? *See p 7, bullet ④.*

② ★ **King's Chapel Burying Ground.** The oldest cemetery in Boston, this little graveyard was established shortly after the settlement, in 1630. Buried here are many of Boston's earliest residents, including the first colonial governor, John Winthrop, and Mary Chilton, the first woman to come ashore in Plymouth in 1620. The graves of William Dawes, Paul Revere's counterpart who rode to Lexington and Concord on the night of April 18, 1775, and Elizabeth Pain, reputedly the model for Hester Prynne in *The Scarlet Letter,* are here, too. The Puritan burying ground gained an Anglican neighbor in 1686, when King's Chapel was established for British officers (it became Unitarian after the Revolution). The current chapel dates to 1749 and is the country's oldest church in continuous use as well as its oldest major stone building. Designed by Peter Harrison, the architect of Christ Church in Cambridge, King's Chapel was constructed by erecting the

Detail of a headstone at King's Chapel.

granite building around its wooden predecessor, then removing the old chapel. *58 Tremont St. (School St.)* ☎ *617/227-2155. www.kings-chapel.org. $2 donation suggested. Chapel year-round Sat 10am–4pm; summer Mon 10am–4pm, Tues–Wed 1–4pm, & Thurs–Fri 10am–4pm. Burying ground daily 8am–5:30pm (until 3pm in winter). Double-check hours on website. T: Green or Blue Line to Government Center.*

🖙 ★ **Lulu's Bake Shoppe.** Colorful and aromatic, Lulu's is a closet-sized bakery—the single table seats two—that's known for its cupcakes. The comic-strip character Little Lulu, the shop's namesake, watches as you order. *227 Hanover St. (Cross St.).* ☎ *617/720-2200. $.*

❹ ★ **Copp's Hill Burying Ground.** Boston didn't set aside a second cemetery until 1659, when this graveyard was established. The site distinguishes this burying ground—it's in a residential neighborhood, and the location, at the crest of Copp's Hill, translates to lovely views of Charlestown and the harbor. As in Boston's other colonial cemeteries, the grave markers alone are worth a trip. The family plot of the prominent Puritan ministers Increase Mather (who was also president of Harvard) and Cotton Mather (Increase's son) is here, as is the grave of Robert Newman, famous today as the sexton of the Old North Church in 1775 (he hung the lanterns that signified "two if by sea"). Phillis Wheatley, a poet and freed slave who was America's first published black author, is believed to have been buried here in an unmarked grave. The graves of many slaves and free blacks are here; Boston's first black neighborhood was nearby, and an estimated 1,000 of the 10,000 or so people buried here over the years were black. The best known is Prince Hall, who fought at Bunker Hill and later founded the first black Masonic lodge. *Hull St. (Salem and Snowhill sts.). Daily 9am–5pm (until 3pm in winter). T: Green or Orange Line to North Station.*

🖙 ★★ **Boston Beanstock Coffee Co.** The only serious competition for the North End's espresso palaces, Boston Beanstock is a lively cafe with tasty salads and sandwiches, free wireless Internet, and, yes, excellent coffee. *97 Salem St. (Wiget St., between Cross and Parmenter sts.).* ☎ *617/742-0040. $.* ●

6

The Best **Dining**

Dining Best Bets

Best **Seafood**
★★★ Legal Sea Foods $$$ 255 State St. (p 109)

Best **Old-Time Boston Experience**
★★★ Durgin-Park $$–$$$ 340 Faneuil Hall Marketplace (p 107)

Best **Pizza**
★★ Pizzeria Regina $ 11½ Thacher St. (p 111)

Best **Vegetarian**
★ Buddha's Delight $ 3 Beach St. (p 106)

Best **for Business**
★★ Locke-Ober $$$$ 3 Winter Place (p 110)

Best **Burgers**
★★ Mr. Bartley's Burger Cottage $ 1246 Massachusetts Ave., Cambridge (p 17)

Best **Raw Bar**
★ Ye Olde Union Oyster House $$$ 41 Union St. (p 112)

Best **When Money Is No Object**
★★★ L'Espalier $$$$ 30 Gloucester St. (p 109)

Best **Down-Home Italian**
★ La Summa $$ 30 Fleet St. (p 109)

Best **Fancy Italian**
★★★ Mamma Maria $$$$ 3 North Sq. (p 110)

Best **Brunch**
★★ S&S Restaurant $–$$ 1334 Cambridge St., Cambridge (p 111)

Best **Mediterranean**
★ Caffè Umbra $$$ 1395 Washington St. (p 106)

Most **Romantic**
★★ UpStairs on the Square $$$$ 91 Winthrop St., Cambridge (p 112)

Best **Sushi**
★ Ginza Japanese Restaurant $$$ 14 Hudson St. (p 108)

Best **Dim Sum**
★ Empire Garden Restaurant $ 690–698 Washington St. (p 107)

Best **Clam Shack**
★★ Jasper White's Summer Shack $$$ 50 Dalton St. (p 109)

Most **Unusual Combo**
★ The Elephant Walk $$ 900 Beacon St. (p 107)

Most Delicious **Cholesterol Infusion**
★ Midwest Grill $$ 1124 Cambridge St., Cambridge (p 110)

Durgin-Park serves up oysters, Boston baked beans, and other New England classics.

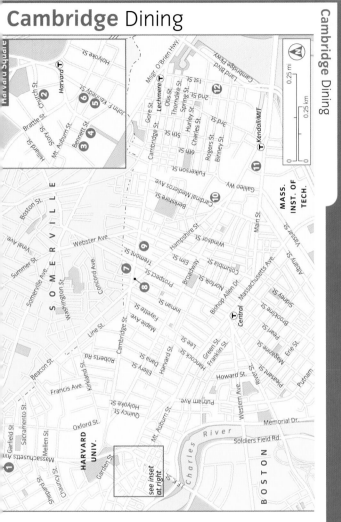

Cambridge Dining

Harvard Square

Harvard

MASS. INST. OF TECH.

HARVARD UNIV.

see inset at right

Charles River

BOSTON

The Blue Room **10**
Bombay Club **5**
Border Café **2**
East Coast Grill & Raw Bar **7**
The Helmand **12**
Legal Sea Foods
(Charles Hotel) **3**
(Kendall Square) **11**
Midwest Grill **9**
Redbones **1**
Rialto **4**
S&S Restaurant **8**
Upstairs on the Square **6**

Boston Dining

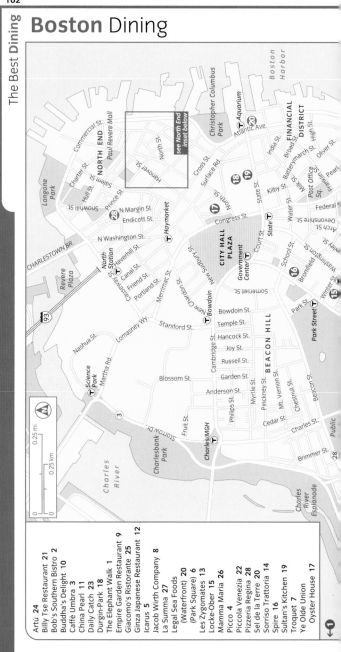

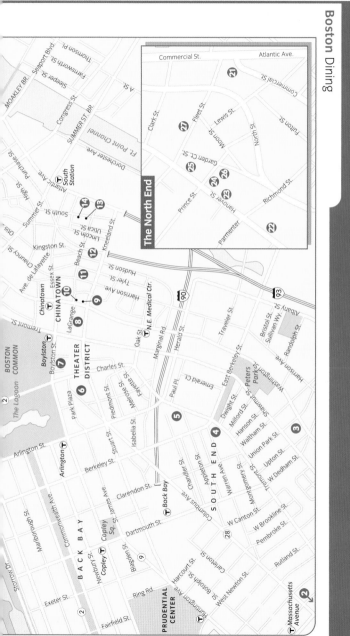

Back Bay Dining

Boston Dining **A to Z**

★ **kids Artú.** NORTH END *ITALIAN* Three storefronts on the Freedom Trail make up this neighborhood favorite, which serves terrific sandwiches, pastas, and roasted meats. *6 Prince St. (Hanover St. and North Sq.)* ☎ *617/742-4336. Entrees $5–$18. AE, MC, V. Lunch & dinner daily. T: Green or Orange Line to Haymarket. Map p 102.*

★ **Bangkok City.** BACK BAY *THAI* The best Thai restaurant in town serves a huge variety of curries as well as excellent takes on the usual noodle dishes. *167 Massachusetts Ave. (Haviland St.)* ☎ *617/266-8884. Entrees $8–$17. AE, DC, DISC, MC, V. Lunch & dinner daily (opens at 3pm Sun). T: Green Line B, C, or D to Hynes/ICA. Map p 104.*

★ **Billy Tse Restaurant.** NORTH END *CHINESE/SUSHI* A Chinese restaurant in an Italian neighborhood is already noteworthy; this one's good, too—as is the sushi bar. *240 Commercial St. (Fleet St.)* ☎ *617/227-9990. Entrees $7–$23. AE, DC, DISC, MC, V. Lunch & dinner daily. T: Blue Line to Aquarium. Map p 102.*

Plenty of Boston restaurants serve up fresh seafood. Try Legal Sea Foods or Ye Olde Union Oyster House for some of the best.

★★★ **The Blue Room.** CAMBRIDGE *ECLECTIC* This subterranean restaurant is a hit thanks to seasonal local ingredients, dynamic seasoning, and flavor-enhancing cooking methods (braising, roasting, grilling). Braised cod with littlenecks is one of my favorite dishes anywhere, challenged recently by roasted duck breast with chestnuts, Brussels sprouts, and a port reduction. *1 Kendall Sq. (Hampshire St.)* ☎ *617/494-9034. Entrees $17–$26. AE, DC, DISC, MC, V. Dinner daily, brunch Sun. T: Red Line to Kendall/MIT. Map p 101.*

★ **Bob's Southern Bistro.** SOUTH END *SOUTHERN/CAJUN* Delectable Southern specialties—fried chicken, collard greens, mac and cheese—plus jazz (live on weekends) make Bob's shine. *604 Columbus Ave. (Northampton St.)* ☎ *617/536-6204. Entrees $10–$16. AE, DISC, MC, V. Dinner weekdays, lunch & dinner Sat, brunch & dinner Sun. T: Orange Line to Massachusetts Ave. Map p 102.*

★ **Bombay Club.** CAMBRIDGE *INDIAN* The menu ranges across the subcontinent; hit the lunch buffet to sample a wide variety of specialties. *57 John F. Kennedy St. (Winthrop St.)* ☎ *617/661-8100. Entrees $11–$18; lunch buffet $8 weekdays, $12 weekends. AE, DC, MC, V. Lunch & dinner daily. T: Red Line to Harvard. Map p 101.*

★ **kids Border Café.** CAMBRIDGE *TEX-MEX* The nonstop party, well lubricated with margaritas and beer, overshadows the tasty enchiladas, fajitas, tacos, and such at this longtime Harvard hangout. *32 Church St. (Palmer St.)* ☎ *617/864-6100. Entrees $7–$15. AE, MC, V. Lunch & dinner daily. T: Red Line to Harvard. Map p 101.*

★ **Brasserie Jo.** BACK BAY *FRENCH* A classic brasserie, with long hours and a wide-ranging menu, this restaurant is a delightful pit stop (and open until 1am daily). *120 Huntington Ave. (W. Newton and Garrison sts.), in the Colonnade Hotel Boston.* ☎ *617/425-3240. Entrees $15–$32. AE, DC, DISC, MC, V. Breakfast, lunch & dinner daily. T: Green Line E to Prudential. Map p 104.*

★★ **The Bristol.** BACK BAY *AMERICAN* This upscale hotel dining room and lounge (the formal restaurant is upstairs) serves astoundingly good comfort food. *200 Boylston St. (Arlington St.), in the Four Seasons Hotel.* ☎ *617/351-2037. Entrees $16–$33. AE, DC, DISC, MC, V. Breakfast, lunch, afternoon tea & dinner daily. T: Green Line to Arlington. Map p 104.*

★ **Buddha's Delight.** CHINATOWN *VIETNAMESE/VEGETARIAN* The food here is so flavorful, you might not even notice that the protein is from soybeans and vegetables. The only animal product used here is milk (in some beverages). *3 Beach St., 2nd floor (Washington St.)* ☎ *617/451-2395. Entrees $6–$13. MC, V. Lunch & dinner daily. T: Orange Line to Chinatown. Map p 102.*

★ **Caffè Umbra.** SOUTH END *MEDITERRANEAN* Classic techniques, sunny flavors, and local produce combine splendidly to create the taste and feel of southern Europe. *1395 Washington St. (Union Park)* ☎ *617/867-0707. Entrees $14–$29. AE, DC, DISC, MC, V. Dinner Tues–Sun. T: Silver Line bus to Union Park. Map p 102.*

★ **Casa Romero.** BACK BAY *MEXICAN* Authentic cuisine served in the intimate dining room or lovely garden makes a meal here feel almost like a trip south of the border. *30 Gloucester St. (Newbury St.)* ☎ *617/536-4341. Entrees $14–$27. AE, DISC, MC, V. Dinner Mon–Sat, brunch & dinner Sun. T: Green Line B, C, or D to Hynes/ICA. Map p 104.*

★★★ kids **China Pearl.** CHINATOWN *CHINESE* One of the city's top dim sum destinations, China Pearl is also popular with groups and families for dinner. *9 Tyler St., 2nd floor (Beach St.)* ☎ *617/426-4338. Entrees $7–$19. AE, MC, V. Breakfast, lunch & dinner daily. T: Orange Line to Chinatown. Map p 102.*

★ **Daily Catch.** NORTH END *SEAFOOD/ITALIAN* Follow the aroma of garlic to this tiny storefront, where the specialty is calamari (squid) and everything is delicious. *323 Hanover St. (Prince St.)* ☎ *617/523-8567. Entrees $12–$19. No credit cards. Lunch & dinner daily. T: Green or Orange Line to Haymarket. Map p 102.*

Festive Casa Romero serves up excellent Mexican cuisine.

Feeling adventurous? Try Daily Catch's delicious squid meatballs.

★★★ kids **Durgin-Park.** FANEUIL HALL MARKETPLACE *NEW ENGLAND* Communal tables give the dining rooms a boardinghouse feel, but they're not terribly noisy—everyone's mouth is full of delicious home-style food. *340 Faneuil Hall Marketplace (Clinton St.)* ☎ *617/227-2038. Entrees $10–$25. AE, DC, DISC, MC, V. Lunch & dinner daily. T: Green or Blue Line to Government Center. Map p 102.*

★★ kids **East Coast Grill & Raw Bar.** CAMBRIDGE *SEAFOOD/BARBE-CUE* This place is a riot—of colors, flavors, and fun. It's been one of the best seafood restaurants in New England for over 2 decades. *1271 Cambridge St. (Prospect and Hampshire sts.)* ☎ *617/491-6568. Entrees $14–$30. AE, MC, V. Dinner daily, brunch Sun. T: Red Line to Central, 10-min. walk. Map p 101.*

★ **The Elephant Walk.** BACK BAY *FRENCH/CAMBODIAN* French on one side, Cambodian on the other, this is the most interesting menu in Boston—with some of the tastiest food. *900 Beacon St. (Park Dr.)* ☎ *617/247-1500. Entrees $11–$27. AE, DC, DISC, MC, V. Lunch weekdays, brunch Sun, dinner daily. T: Green Line C to St. Mary's St. Map p 102.*

★ kids **Empire Garden Restaurant.** CHINATOWN *CHINESE* The best dim sum in town is here, in a huge converted theater that's especially busy at midday on weekends. Dinner is mostly Cantonese. *690–698 Washington St. (Kneeland and Beach sts.)* ☎ *617/482-8898. Entrees $9–$23. MC, V. Breakfast, lunch & dinner daily. T: Orange Line to Chinatown. Map p 102.*

★★ **Giacomo's Ristorante.** NORTH END *ITALIAN/SEAFOOD* The line is long, the dining room is small, and the food is worth the trouble. Be sure to check the specials board, where the kitchen does some of its best work. *355 Hanover St. (Fleet St.)* ☎ *617/523-9026. Entrees $14–$21. No credit cards. Dinner daily. T: Green or Orange Line to Haymarket. Map p 102.*

Durgin-Park is the best place in the city to try Boston baked beans.

Jacob Wirth Company has been serving Bostonians since 1868.

★ **Ginza Japanese Restaurant.**
CHINATOWN *JAPANESE* Kimono-clad waitresses serve Boston's best sushi at this out-of-the-way restaurant. It's open daily until at least 2am. *14 Hudson St. (Kneeland and Beach sts.)* ☎ *617/338-2261. Entrees $11–$20. AE, DC, MC, V. Lunch & dinner daily. T: Orange Line to New England Medical Center. Map p 102.*

★ **Grill 23 & Bar.** BACK BAY *STEAKS* The city's top steakhouse is a magnet for the high-rolling, deal-making set. I could make a meal of the toothsome a la carte side dishes. *161 Berkeley St. (Stuart St.)* ☎ *617/542-2255. Entrees $21–$44. AE, DC, DISC, MC, V. Dinner daily. T: Green Line to Arlington. Map p 104.*

★ **The Helmand.** CAMBRIDGE *AFGHAN* The cuisine at this elegant restaurant combines elements of Indian, Pakistani, and Middle Eastern food to good effect. It's flavorful, filling (but not heavy), and vegetarian friendly. *143 First St. (Bent St.)*

☎ *617/492-4646. Entrees $13–$21. AE, MC, V. Dinner daily. T: Green Line to Lechmere. Map p 101.*

★★ **Icarus.** SOUTH END *ECLECTIC* A long-time favorite in a finicky city, this romantic restaurant uses the finest New England ingredients and Continental techniques in its delicious cuisine. There's live jazz in the bar on Friday. *3 Appleton St. (Tremont St.)* ☎ *617/426-1790. Entrees $26–$36. AE, DC, DISC, MC, V. Dinner daily. T: Green Line to Arlington. Map p 102.*

★ **Jacob Wirth Company.** THEATER DISTRICT *GERMAN/AMERICAN* The long bar and wooden floor suggest a vintage saloon, and rib-sticking specialties like wursts and Wiener schnitzel share the menu with comfort food like chicken pot pie. *31–37 Stuart St. (Tremont St.)* ☎ *617/338-8586. Entrees $7–$27. AE, DC, DISC, MC, V. Lunch &*

Jasper White's serves up lobster in preparations both humble (rolls) and gourmet (pan roasted with herbs).

dinner Tues–Sun. T: Green Line to Boylston. Map p 102.

★★ kids **Jasper White's Summer Shack.** BACK BAY *SEAFOOD* The Summer Shack feels like a casual seaside place (think corn dogs, lobster rolls, and fried clams) and tastes like the brainchild of a gourmet chef—because it is (think pan-roasted lobster with chervil and chives). *50 Dalton St. (Boylston and Belvedere sts.)* ☎ *617/867-9955. Entrees $12–$35. AE, DISC, MC, V. Lunch weekdays, brunch weekends, dinner daily. T: Green Line B, C, or D to Hynes/ICA. Map p 104.*

★ **La Summa.** NORTH END *ITALIAN* A neighborhood native owns and runs La Summa, a friendly place where many specialties are family recipes; try the handmade pasta. *30 Fleet St. (Hanover and North sts.)* ☎ *617/523-9503. Entrees $11–$24. AE, DC, DISC, MC, V. Dinner daily. T: Green or Orange Line to Haymarket. Map p 102.*

★★★ kids **Legal Sea Foods.** WATERFRONT *SEAFOOD* I'd love to point you to a hole-in-the-wall and say, "There's the secret place that only the locals know about—it's the best seafood restaurant in the Boston area." But I can't. Legal's is no secret, but it is the best. *255 State St. (Atlantic Ave.)* ☎ *617/227-3115. Entrees $14–$35. AE, DC, DISC, MC, V. Lunch & dinner daily. T: Blue Line to Aquarium. Branches: Prudential Center, 800 Boylston St. (Fairfield*

Legal Sea Food's exceptional wine list complements the best seafood in Boston.

St.), ☎ *617/266-6800, T: Green Line B, C, or D to Hynes/ICA; Park Sq., 36 Park Place (Columbus Ave. and Stuart St.),* ☎ *617/426-4444, T: Green Line to Arlington; Copley Place, 100 Huntington Ave. (Dartmouth St.), 2nd level,* ☎ *617/266-7775, T: Orange Line to Back Bay; Charles Hotel, 20 University Rd. (Bennett St.), Cambridge,* ☎ *617/491-9400, T: Red Line to Harvard; 5 Cambridge Center (Main and Ames sts.),* ☎ *617/864-3400, T: Red Line to Kendall/MIT. Maps p 101, 102, and 104.*

★★★ **L'Espalier.** BACK BAY *FRENCH* The Boston area's foremost special-occasion restaurant is a formal place with a magnificent, ever-changing menu and wine list. *30 Gloucester St. (Newbury St.)* ☎ *617/262-3023. 3-course prix fixe $75. AE, DC, DISC, MC, V. Dinner Mon–Sat. T: Green Line B, C, or D to Hynes/ICA. Map p 104.*

★★ **Les Zygomates.** LEATHER DISTRICT *FRENCH* A bistro and

The Elephant Walk.

L'Espalier's menu changes often, but never disappoints.

wine bar, Les Zygomates (lay *zig-o-mat*) serves classic, casual dishes in two dining rooms; one has live jazz at night. *129 South St. (Tufts and Beach sts.)* ☎ *617/542-5108. Entrees $18–$26. AE, DC, DISC, MC, V. Lunch weekdays, dinner Mon–Sat. T: Red Line to South Station. Map p 102.*

★★ **Locke-Ober.** DOWNTOWN CROSSING *CONTINENTAL* Traditional but not stuffy, Locke-Ober is a classic Boston destination—it looks like a wood-paneled men's club—updated for the 21st century. *3 Winter Place (Winter and Washington sts.)* ☎ *617/542-1340. Entrees $28–$49. AE, DISC, MC, V. Lunch weekdays, dinner Mon–Sat. T: Red or Orange Line to Downtown Crossing. Map p 102.*

★★★ **Mamma Maria.** NORTH END *NORTHERN ITALIAN* My favorite North End restaurant serves creative cuisine in a romantic town house. The best dish is *osso buco,* and anything with seafood is wonderful. *3 North Sq. (Prince and Garden Court sts.)* ☎ *617/523-0077. Entrees $24–$35. AE, DC, DISC, MC, V. Dinner daily. T: Green or Orange Line to Haymarket. Map p 102.*

You'll find some of the North End's best pizza at Pizzeria Regina.

★★ **kids Midwest Grill.** CAMBRIDGE *BRAZILIAN Rodizio,* or Brazilian barbecue, is a sort of buffet—but the food comes to you. On swords. Waiters serve succulent pork, lamb, beef, sausage, and chicken cooked over an open fire until you ask them to stop. You serve yourself side dishes. *1124 Cambridge St. (Norfolk and Elm sts.)* ☎ *617/354-7536. Rodizio $24 at dinner, $18 at lunch. AE, DISC, MC, V. Lunch & dinner daily. T: Red Line to Central, 15-min. walk. Map p 101.*

★ **kids Picco.** SOUTH END *PIZZA* It's all in the name, which is short for "Pizza and Ice Cream Company." The excellent pizza arrives steaming from the wood-burning oven; the ice cream is a perfect chaser. *513 Tremont St. (E. Berkeley and Clarendon sts.)* ☎ *617/927-0066. Pizza $10–$20. MC, V. Lunch & dinner daily. T: Orange Line to Back Bay. Map p 102.*

★ **Piccola Venezia.** NORTH END *ITALIAN* A lively, reliable spot right on the Freedom Trail, this is my go-to place for Italian-American specialties like lasagna and spaghetti and meatballs. *263 Hanover St. (Cross and Richmond sts.)* ☎ *617/523-3888. Entrees $12–$22. AE, DISC, MC, V. Lunch & dinner daily. T: Green or Orange Line to Haymarket. Map p 102.*

★★ kids **Pizzeria Regina.** NORTH END *PIZZA* That picture you have in your head of a neighborhood pizza place in an old-time Italian neighborhood? This is it. *11½ Thacher St. (North Margin St.)* ☎ *617/227-0765. Pizza $11–$17. No credit cards. Lunch & dinner daily. T: Green or Orange Line to Haymarket. Map p 102.*

★ kids **Redbones.** SOMERVILLE *BARBECUE* I'm sending you off the tourist trail, but it's an easy detour, and I promise you won't be sorry: Redbones serves the best barbecue (and all the trimmings) in the Boston area. *55 Chester St. (Elm St.)* ☎ *617/ 628-2000. Entrees $6–$19. No credit cards. Lunch & dinner daily. T: Red Line to Davis. Map p 101.*

★★ **Rialto.** CAMBRIDGE *MEDITER-RANEAN* In much the same way that the Charles is the quintessential Cambridge hotel, Rialto is the city's premier special-occasion dining destination. It's elegant yet a little funky—another quintessentially Cambridge quality (for elegant verging on stately, stay on the Boston side of the river and head to L'Espalier). Everything at Rialto is just so, starting with the luscious cuisine. *1 Bennett St. (Eliot St.), in the Charles Hotel.* ☎ *617/661-5050. Entrees $23–$43. AE, DC, MC, V. Dinner daily. T: Red Line to Harvard. Map p 101.*

★★ kids **S&S Restaurant.** CAM-BRIDGE *DELI* The best weekend-brunch restaurant in the Boston area serves classic deli food all week. *1334 Cambridge St. (Prospect and Hampshire sts.)* ☎ *617/354-0777. Entrees $4–$15. AE, MC, V. Breakfast, lunch & dinner daily;*

brunch weekends. T: Red Line to Central, 10-min. walk. Map p 101.

★ kids **Sebastian's Map Room Café.** BACK BAY *LIGHT FARE* A retreat from the Back Bay's pandemonium, Sebastian's serves tasty soups, salads, sandwiches, and sweets. And you get to talk in a library. *700 Boylston St. (Dartmouth St.), in the Boston Public Library.* ☎ *617/385-5660. Entrees $5–$8. No credit cards. Breakfast & lunch Mon–Sat. T: Green Line to Copley. Map p 104.*

★★ **Sel de la Terre.** WATER-FRONT *FRENCH* Provençal flavors raise seasonal local ingredients to a new level. I've never had a disappointing fish dish here, and carnivorous friends swear by the steak frites. *255 State St. (Atlantic Ave.)* ☎ *617/720-1300. Entrees $26. AE, DC, DISC, MC, V. Lunch & dinner daily. T: Blue Line to Aquarium. Map p 102.*

★ **Sorriso Trattoria.** LEATHER DISTRICT *ITALIAN* Pizza and sandwiches at lunch, Italian classics at dinner, and a chic yet welcoming space are a good fit in this funky neighborhood. *107 South St. (Tufts*

Sebastian's Map Room Café.

and Beach sts.) ☎ 617/259-1560. *Entrees $16–$24. AE, DC, DISC, MC, V. Lunch weekdays, dinner Mon–Sat. T: Red Line to South Station. Map p 102.*

★★ **Spire.** DOWNTOWN CROSSING *NEW ENGLAND* Creative versions of classic dishes, inventively prepared and presented (soups are poured at the table), put this elegant restaurant on the map. *90 Tremont St. (Bromfield St.), in the Nine Zero hotel.* ☎ 617/772-0202. *Entrees $23–$39. AE, DC, DISC, MC, V. Lunch weekdays, brunch weekends, dinner daily. T: Red or Green Line to Park St. Map p 102.*

★ kids **Stephanie's on Newbury.** BACK BAY *AMERICAN* "Sophisticated comfort food" is the calling card of this neighborhood favorite, which has a lively sidewalk seating area. *190 Newbury St. (Exeter St.)* ☎ 617/236-0990. *Entrees $14–$35. AE, DC, DISC, MC, V. Lunch & dinner daily. T: Green Line to Copley. Map p 104.*

★★ **Sultan's Kitchen.** FINANCIAL DISTRICT *TURKISH* Mostly a takeout place with a businesslike clientele, Sultan's Kitchen is perfect for a picnic. It has a few tables where you can enjoy the delectable Middle Eastern specialties and a rainbow of salads. *116 State St. (Broad St.)* ☎ 617/728-2828. *Entrees $6–$12. AE, MC, V. Lunch Mon–Sat. T: Blue Line to Aquarium. Map p 102.*

★★ **Tapéo.** BACK BAY *SPANISH* A perfect place for a celebration, Tapéo specializes in tapas, flavorful appetizer-like bites that go well with sangria. *266 Newbury St. (Fairfield and Gloucester sts.)* ☎ 617/267-4799. *Entrees $19–$25, tapas $5–$10. AE, DC, MC, V. Dinner daily. T: Green Line B, C, or D to Hynes/ICA. Map p 104.*

★★ **Troquet.** THEATER DISTRICT *NEW AMERICAN* Wine is the focus here; the subtly flavorful seasonal cuisine complements the daily selections from the extensive wine list. *140 Boylston St. (Tremont and S. Charles sts.)* ☎ 617/695-9463. *Entrees $26–$38. AE, DC, DISC, MC, V. Dinner daily in lounge, Tues–Sat in dining room. T: Green Line to Boylston. Map p 102.*

★★ **UpStairs on the Square.** CAMBRIDGE *ECLECTIC* The second-floor dining room, known as the Monday Club Bar, is a cozy destination for upscale comfort food. *91 Winthrop St. (Kennedy and Eliot sts.)* ☎ 617/864-1933. *Entrees $11–$26. AE, DC, DISC, MC, V. Lunch weekdays, brunch Sun, dinner daily. T: Red Line to Harvard. Map p 101.*

★ kids **Ye Olde Union Oyster House.** FANEUIL HALL MARKETPLACE *SEAFOOD* The country's oldest restaurant (since 1826) is on the Freedom Trail—tourist central—but very popular with locals. *41 Union St. (North and Hanover sts.)* ☎ 617/227-2750. *Entrees $17–$29. AE, DC, DISC, MC, V. Lunch & dinner daily. T: Orange or Green Line to Haymarket. Map p 102.* ●

Ye Olde Union Oyster House is the perfect place to try clam chowder or oyster stew.

Nightlife Best Bets

Best **Views**
★★★ Top of the Hub, *Prudential Center, 800 Boylston St. (p 122)*

Best **Alfresco Pickup Joint**
★ Tia's, *200 Atlantic Ave. (p 119)*

Best **Martinis**
★★ The Bar at the Ritz-Carlton, *15 Arlington St. (p 118)*

Best **Upscale Pool Hall**
★★ Flat Top Johnny's, *1 Kendall Sq., Cambridge (p 122)*

Best **Irish Pub**
★★ Mr. Dooley's Boston Tavern, *77 Broad St. (p 122)*

Best **Gay Scene**
★★ 209 at Club Café, *209 Columbus Ave. (p 120)*

Best **Deal**
★★ Toad, *1912 Massachusetts Ave., Cambridge (p 121)*

Best **Scorpion Bowls**
★ The Hong Kong, *1238 Massachusetts Ave., Cambridge (p 118)*

Most **Worth the Trip**
★★★ Johnny D's Uptown Restaurant & Music Club, *17 Holland St., Somerville (p 121)*

Best **Place to Meet Politicians**
★ 21st Amendment, *150 Bowdoin St. (p 119)*

Best **Folk Club**
★★★ Club Passim, *47 Palmer St., Cambridge (p 121)*

Best **Rock Club**
★★★ The Middle East, *472–480 Massachusetts Ave., Cambridge (p 121)*

Best **Dance Club**
★★★ Avalon, *15 Lansdowne St. (p 119)*

Best **Comedy Club**
★★ The Comedy Studio, *1238 Massachusetts Ave., Cambridge (p 119)*

Best **Old-School Jazz Club**
★ Wally's Cafe, *427 Massachusetts Ave. (p 120)*

Best **Upscale Jazz Clubs**
★★★ Regattabar, *1 Bennett St., Cambridge (p 120)*; and ★★★ Scullers Jazz Club, *400 Soldiers Field Rd. (p 120)*

Best **Old-School Sports Bar**
★★ The Fours, *166 Canal St. (p 122)*

Best **Yuppie Sports Bar**
★ Game On! Sports Café, *82 Lansdowne St. (p 122)*

Soak in the skyline at Top of the Hub.

Cambridge Nightlife

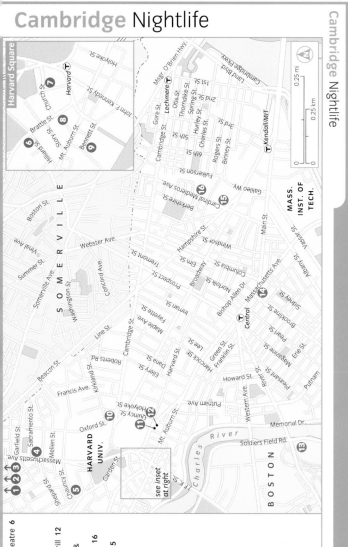

Harvard Square

American Repertory Theatre 6
Brattle Theatre 8
Club Passim 7
The Comedy Studio 11
Flat Top Johnny's 15
Grafton Street Pub & Grill 12
The Hong Kong 11
Johnny D's Restaurant &
Music Club 2
Kendall Square Cinema 16
Lizard Lounge 4
Longy School of Music 5
The Middle East 14
Regattabar 9
Sanders Theatre 10
Scullers Jazz Club 13
Somerville Theatre 1
Toad 3

Boston Nightlife

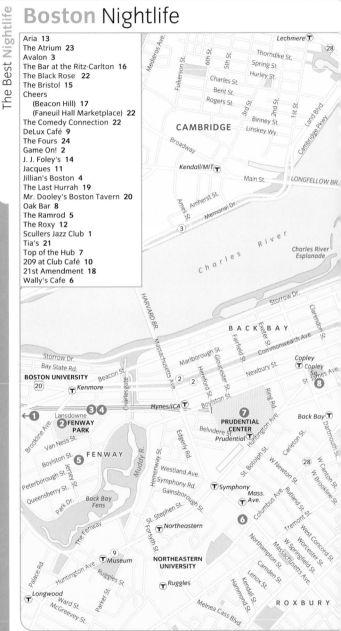

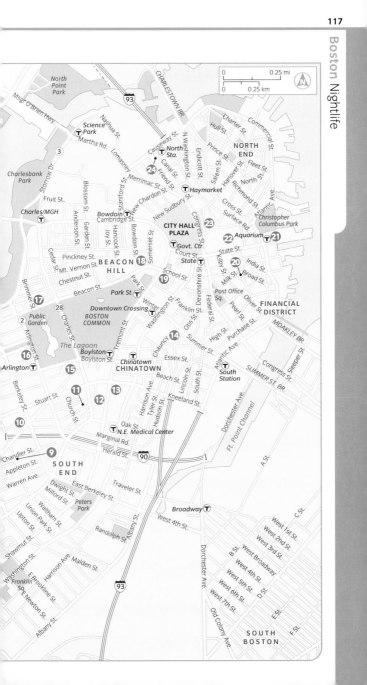

North Point Park

Msgr O'Brien Hwy.

CHARLESTOWN BR.

0   0.25 mi
0   0.25 km

Science Park Ⓣ

Nashua St.

93

Martha Rd.

Lomasney Way

Charlesbank Park

3

Storrow Dr.

Causeway St.

North Sta. Ⓣ

24

Canal St.

Friend St.

Merrimac St.

N Washington St.

Endicott St.

Charter St.

Commercial St.

Hull St.

Prince St.

N Bennet St.

NORTH END

Fleet St.

Fruit St.

Blossom St.

Staniford St.

New Chardon St.

Hanover St.

Richmond St.

North St.

Charles/MGH Ⓣ

Cambridge St.

Bowdoin St.

Ⓣ Bowdoin

Anderson St.

Garden St.

Joy St.

Hancock St.

Bowdoin St.

Somerset St.

New Sudbury St.

Ⓣ Haymarket

Cross St.

Surface Rd.

Atlantic Ave.

Christopher Columbus Park

CITY HALL PLAZA

23

Cedar St.

Mt. Vernon St.

Pinckney St.

BEACON HILL

18

Ⓣ Govt. Ctr.

Court St.

State Ⓣ

Congress St.

State St.

Kilby St.

India St.

22

Aquarium Ⓣ

21

Brimmer St.

Chestnut St.

Park St.

Beacon St.

Park St. Ⓣ

19

School St.

Devonshire St.

Milk St.

Broad St.

20

FINANCIAL DISTRICT

Charles St.

17

Public Garden

2

28

Arlington St.

The Lagoon

Downtown Crossing Ⓣ

BOSTON COMMON

Winter St.

Washington St.

Franklin St.

Otis St.

Federal St.

Pearl St.

High St.

Oliver St.

Purchase St.

Post Office Sq.

MOAKLEY BR.

Congress St.

Sleeper St.

Arlington Ⓣ

16

Boylston Ⓣ

Boylston St.

15

Tremont St.

Chinatown Ⓣ

CHINATOWN

Chauncy St.

14

Summer St.

Essex St.

Beach St.

Atlantic Ave.

South Station Ⓣ

SUMMER ST. BR.

Berkeley St.

Stuart St.

11

Church St.

12

13

Harrison Ave.

Tyler St.

Hudson St.

Lincoln St.

South St.

Kneeland St.

Dorchester Ave.

Ft. Point Channel

10

Oak St.

N.E. Medical Center Ⓣ

Marginal Rd.

Herald St.

90

A St.

Chandler St.

9

Appleton St.

Warren Ave.

SOUTH END

East Berkeley St.

Dwight St.

Milford St.

Waltham St.

Union Park St.

Upton St.

Peters Park

Traveler St.

Broadway Ⓣ

West 4th St.

C St.

West 1st St.

West 2nd St.

West Broadway

West 3rd St.

B St.

West 4th St.

Shawmut St.

Washington St.

E Brookline St.

Harrison Ave.

Malden St.

Randolph St.

Albany St.

West 5th St.

D St.

West 6th St.

West 7th St.

Franklin Sq.

Newton St.

Albany St.

93

Dorchester Ave.

Old Colony Ave.

SOUTH BOSTON

E St.

F St.

Boston Nightlife A to Z

Bars

★★ The Bar at the Ritz-Carlton BACK BAY   This classic aristocratic watering hole is a cozy, paneled room with a power-broker clientele, a baronial fireplace, a view of the Public Garden, and killer martinis. *15 Arlington St. (Newbury St.)* ☎ *617/536-5700. T: Green Line to Arlington. Map p 116.*

Cheers BEACON HILL & FANEUIL HALL MARKETPLACE   The bar that inspired the TV show was a fun neighborhood place called the Bull & Finch. Now it's called Cheers (bring a camera—the sign is outside), and although it's still fun, the neighborhood atmosphere is pretty much gone. There's another Cheers at Faneuil Hall that faithfully replicates the set of the TV show and unabashedly caters to the tourist hordes. *84 Beacon St. (Brimmer St.)* ☎ *617/227-9605. www.cheers boston.com. T: Green Line to Arlington. Map p 116. Faneuil Hall branch: Quincy Market Building, South Canopy.* ☎ *617/227-0150. T: Green or Blue Line to Government Center. Map p 116.*

★★ DeLux Café SOUTH END   The awesome decor—posters, postcards, album covers (from LPs!), and such— makes a perfect backdrop for the cool neighborhood crowd, microbrew selection, and veggie-friendly ethnic food. *100 Chandler St. (Clarendon St.)* ☎ *617/338-5258. T: Orange Line to Back Bay. Map p 116.*

★ The Hong Kong CAMBRIDGE   The upstairs bar at this retro Chinese restaurant is a Harvard hangout that inspires the question: How do these kids suck down all those scorpion bowls and stay so smart? *1238 Massachusetts Ave. (Plympton and Bow sts.)* ☎ *617/864-5311. T: Red Line to Harvard. Map p 115.*

★ J. J. Foley's DOWNTOWN CROSSING   The epitome of a divey after-work bar, Foley's is a big, noisy place with a top-notch beer menu and an excellent jukebox. Plan to eat somewhere else. *21 Kingston St. (Summer and Bedford sts.)* ☎ *617/ 338-7713. T: Red or Orange Line to Downtown Crossing. Map p 116.*

★★ The Last Hurrah DOWNTOWN CROSSING   The Parker House's 19th-century atmosphere extends to the lobby bar, which is popular with the after-work crowd as well as Beacon Hill political types. *60 School St. (Tremont St.), in the Omni Parker House hotel.* ☎ *617/ 725-1888. T: Green or Blue Line to Government Center. Map p 116.*

Cheers at Faneuil Hall.

Avalon's cavernous multilevel space includes a concert stage, private booths, and large dance floors.

★★ **Oak Bar** BACK BAY Wood-paneled and clubby, with leather seating and a raw bar, the Oak Bar is an oasis of calm in the frenzy of Copley Square. No jeans, shorts, or sneakers. *138 St. James Ave. (Clarendon St.), in the Fairmont Copley Plaza Hotel.* ☎ *617/267-5300. T: Green Line to Copley. Map p 116.*

★ **Tia's** WATERFRONT In warm weather, the huge patio a stone's throw from the Financial District is the busiest after-work meet market in town. *200 Atlantic Ave. (State St.), next to the Boston Marriott Long Wharf hotel.* ☎ *617/227-0828. www.tiaswaterfront.com. T: Blue Line to Aquarium. Map p 116.*

★ **21st Amendment** BEACON HILL Across the street from the State House, the 21st Amendment is a neighborhood bar in a politico-infested neighborhood. (The actual 21st Amendment repealed Prohibition—get it?) *150 Bowdoin St. (Beacon St.)* ☎ *617/227-7100. T: Red or Green Line to Park St. Map p 116.*

Comedy Clubs
★ **The Comedy Connection** FANEUIL HALL MARKETPLACE This is the place to see established comics, especially on weekends; up-and-coming locals get their shot earlier in the week. *245 Quincy Market Place, 2nd floor.* ☎ *617/248-9700. www.comedyconnectionboston.com. Tickets $15–$45. T: Green or Blue Line to Government Center. Map p 116.*

★★ **The Comedy Studio** CAMBRIDGE A hilarious proving ground for up-and-coming comics, who complement stand-up with sketches and improv, the Comedy Studio is no secret to network scouts. *1238 Massachusetts Ave. (Plympton and Bow sts.)* ☎ *617/661-6507. www.the comedystudio.com. Cover $6–$10. T: Red Line to Harvard. Map p 115.*

Dance Clubs
★ **Aria** THEATER DISTRICT This little subterranean retreat feels like a lounge and sounds like a cutting-edge iPod. Aria attracts a sophisticated, late-20s-and-up crowd. Thursday is gay night. *246 Tremont St. (Stuart St.), in the Wilbur Theatre.* ☎ *617/338-7080. Cover $10–$20. T: Green Line to Boylston. Map p 116.*

★★★ **Avalon** FENWAY Avalon, the anchor of the nightclub strip across from Fenway Park, is the only Boston-area club that approaches New York's in all-around style. Sunday is gay night. *15 Lansdowne St. (Brookline Ave.)* ☎ *617/262-2424. www.avalonboston.com. Cover $5–$20. T: Green Line D to Fenway. Map p 116.*

Tower of Power and Al Jarreau have played Scullers in recent years.

★★ The Roxy THEATER DISTRICT A diverse slate of DJs attracts serious dancers to this dramatic space, a former hotel ballroom with a stage and a balcony (great for watching the chic crowd). *279 Tremont St. (Stuart St.), in the Courtyard Boston Tremont Hotel.* ☎ *617/338-7699. www.roxyplex.com. Cover $10–$20. T: Green Line to Boylston. Map p 116.*

Gay & Lesbian Bars & Clubs

★ Jacques BAY VILLAGE Boston's only drag club also books performance artists and, on weekends, live music. Bay Village is a tiny neighborhood next to the Theatre District. *79 Broadway (off Charles St. S.)* ☎ *617/436-8902. www.jacques cabaret.com. Cover $5–$10. T: Green Line to Arlington. Map p 116.*

★ The Ramrod FENWAY Upstairs is a bar with a pool table, downstairs is a crowded dance club, leather is required in the back room (jackets don't count), and a cruisey atmosphere prevails throughout. *1254 Boylston St. (Jersey St.)* ☎ *617/266-2986.*

Local and international artists, including Buckwheat Zydeco and Madeline Peyroux, play at Regattabar.

www.ramrodboston.com. T: Green Line D to Fenway. Map p 116.

★★ 209 at Club Café SOUTH END A club, video bar, and restaurant all under one roof, this upscale spot is the city's top gay nightlife destination. Thursday is see-and-be-seen night. *209 Columbus Ave. (Berkeley St.)* ☎ *617/536-0966. www.clubcafe.com. No cover. T: Orange Line to Back Bay. Map p 116.*

Jazz Clubs

★★★ Regattabar CAMBRIDGE A large, elegant room in a swanky hotel, the Regattabar is engaged in a long-running battle with Scullers (see next listing) to book the biggest names in jazz. Everybody wins. *1 Bennett St. (Eliot St.), Cambridge, in the Charles Hotel.* ☎ *617/661-5000. www.regattabarjazz.com. Tickets $12–$40. T: Red Line to Harvard. Map p 115.*

★★★ Scullers Jazz Club ALLSTON Without easy access to the T, Scullers is harder to reach than the Regattabar (see previous listing)—which means these patrons *really* want to be here. *400 Soldiers Field Rd. (Mass. Turnpike Cambridge exit), in the Doubletree Guest Suites hotel.* ☎ *617/562-4111. www.scullersjazz. com. Tickets $15–$50. Map p 115.*

★ Wally's Cafe SOUTH END Hardcore jazz fans have sought out Wally's since it opened in 1947. This small, family-run place books mostly local talent and attracts a serious—and seriously diverse—crowd. *427 Massachusetts Ave. (Columbus Ave.)* ☎ *617/424-1408. No cover. 1-drink minimum. T: Orange Line to Massachusetts Ave. Map p 116.*

Live-Music Clubs

★★★ Club Passim CAMBRIDGE

The place for folk music is a subterranean coffeehouse founded (as Club 47) in 1958. Passim has booked every folk artist you've ever worshiped, and plenty you haven't heard of. Yet. *47 Palmer St. (Church St.)* ☎ *617/492-7679. www.club passim.org. Cover usually $5–$20. T: Red Line to Harvard. Map p 115.*

★★★ Johnny D's Uptown Restaurant & Music Club

SOMERVILLE The impressively varied schedule (rock, blues, bluegrass, and much more) makes this friendly, family-run club well worth the trip— just two stops past Harvard Square. *17 Holland St. (Davis Sq.)* ☎ *617/776-2004. www.johnnyds.com. Cover usually $8–$12. T: Red Line to Davis. Map p 115.*

★★ Lizard Lounge CAMBRIDGE

The "stage" at this subterranean club is on the floor, allowing the rock and folk musicians to stray into the 20- and 30-something crowd. *1667 Massachusetts Ave. (Wendell St.)* ☎ *617/547-0759. www.lizardloungeclub.com. Cover for late shows $5–$12. T: Red Line to Harvard. Map p 115.*

★★★ The Middle East CAMBRIDGE Four performance spaces

The Middle East showcases local bands as well as international talent.

The Bristol is a great choice for a post-theater drink.

and bookers with an uncanny ear for promising alternative and progressive artists make this the best (and possibly loudest) rock club in the Boston area. *472–480 Massachusetts Ave. (Brookline St.)* ☎ *617/864-3278. www.mideastclub.com. Cover $7–$15. T: Red Line to Central. Map p 115.*

★★ Toad CAMBRIDGE Here you'll

find local rock, rockabilly, and blues artists performing for a savvy crowd that appreciates the top-notch entertainment, beer menu, intimate surroundings, and price (free!). *1912 Massachusetts Ave. (Porter Rd.)* ☎ *617/497-4950. www.toad cambridge.com. No cover. T: Red Line to Porter. Map p 115.*

Lounges

★ The Atrium FANEUIL HALL

MARKETPLACE A surprisingly sophisticated space in a touristy area, the Atrium is a comfy spot with huge windows that allow great people-watching. *26 North St. (Clinton St.), at the Millennium Bostonian Hotel.* ☎ *617/523-3600. T: Orange or Green Line to Haymarket. Map p 116.*

★★★ The Bristol BACK BAY The

posh Four Seasons hotel's restaurant and lounge is a magnet for a well-heeled older crowd. There's live jazz piano nightly and, on weekends, a dessert buffet. *200 Boylston St. (Arlington St.), in the Four Seasons Hotel.* ☎ *617/351-2037. T: Green Line to Arlington. Map p 116.*

The Best Nightlife

★★★ **Top of the Hub** BACK BAY The 52nd-floor lounge is a gorgeous setting for romance, especially if you arrive in daylight and watch the sunset. Top of the Hub schedules live jazz nightly. No jeans. *Prudential Center, 800 Boylston St. (Fairfield St.).* ☎ *617/536-1775. T: Green Line E to Prudential. Map p 116.*

Pool Parlors

★★ **Flat Top Johnny's** CAMBRIDGE This casual hangout is a dark, cavernous space with a dozen pool tables and a long menu of microbrews. So cool, yet so close to MIT—go figure. *1 Kendall Sq. (Hampshire St.)* ☎ *617/494-9565. www.flattopjohnnys.com. T: Red Line to Kendall/MIT. Map p 115.*

★ **Jillian's Boston** FENWAY Fifty-two pool tables are the tip of the iceberg—Jillian's is also a bowling alley, dance club, sports bar, and restaurant. Children are admitted, but only during the day. *145 Ipswich St. (Lansdowne St.)* ☎ *617/437-0300. www.jilliansboston.com. T: Green Line D to Fenway. Map p 116.*

Pubs

The Black Rose FANEUIL HALL MARKETPLACE The Black Rose is usually crowded with out-of-towners, but the enthusiastic musicians performing traditional Irish music don't care that the people singing along are mostly tourists. *160 State St. (Commercial St.)* ☎ *617/742-2286. Cover $3–$5. T: Blue Line to Aquarium. Map p 116.*

★ **Grafton Street Pub & Grill** CAMBRIDGE The stylish room, professional crowd, and tasty comfort food make this place a neighborhood standby; I'd go back just for the Irish bartenders and deftly poured Guinness. *1230 Massachusetts Ave. (Bow St.)* ☎ *617/497-0400. T: Red Line to Harvard. Map p 115.*

★★ **Mr. Dooley's Boston Tavern** FINANCIAL DISTRICT This authentically decorated pub is far enough off the tourist track to be a favorite with local office workers and homesick expats. There's live Irish music on weekend nights. *77 Broad St. (Custom House St.)* ☎ *617/338-5656. Cover (Fri–Sat) $3–$5. T: Blue Line to Aquarium. Map p 116.*

Sports Bars

★★ **The Fours** NORTH STATION Across the street from TD Banknorth Garden, the Fours has been a Boston landmark since 1976. It boasts tons of TVs, abundant memorabilia, and a good pub-grub menu. *166 Canal St. (Causeway St.)* ☎ *617/720-4455. T: Green or Orange Line to North Station. Map p 116.*

★ **Game On!** FENWAY If you can't get a ticket to the game, this may be the next-best thing: This high-tech "sports cafe" and its dozens of TVs are actually *in* the ballpark (though there's no access to the stands). *82 Lansdowne St. (Brookline Ave.)* ☎ *617/351-7001. www.gameonboston.com. T: Green Line D to Fenway. Map p 116.* ●

On game days, the line to get into Game On! stretches down the street.

8 The Best Arts & Entertainment

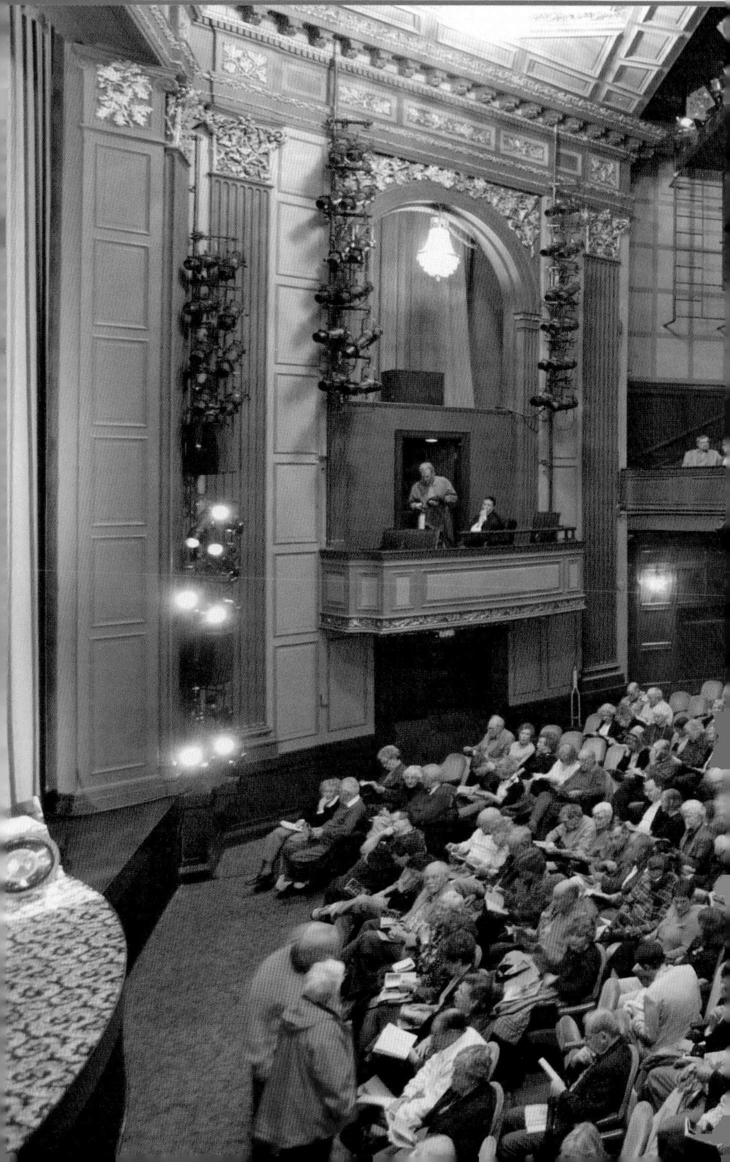

Boston **Arts & Entertainment**

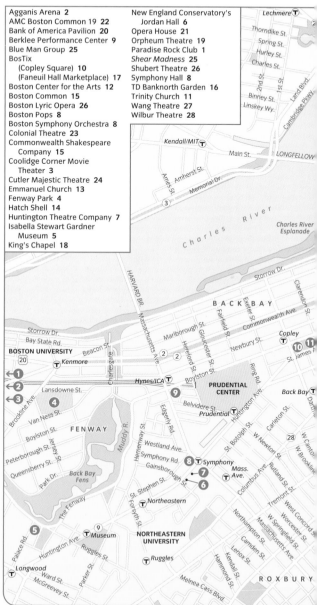

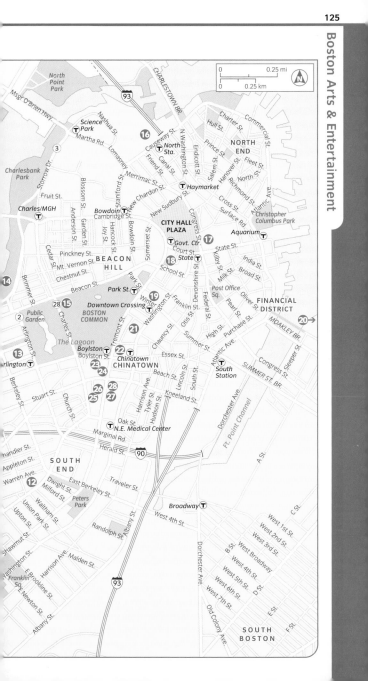

Arts & Entertainment
Best Bets

Best **Concert Hall**
★★ Symphony Hall, *301 Massachusetts Ave. (p 128)*

Best **18th-Century Flashback**
★★ Handel & Haydn Society, *various locations (p 127)*

Best **Concert Venue with a View**
★★ Bank of America Pavilion, *290 Northern Ave. (p 130)*

Most **Beautiful Indoor Venue**
★★ Opera House, *539 Washington St. (p 132)*

Most **Beautiful Outdoor Venues**
★ Boston Landmarks Orchestra, *various locations (p 127)*

Best **Dinner & a Show**
★★ Boston Pops, Symphony Hall, *301 Massachusetts Ave. (p 127)*

Best **Theater Deal**
★★ Commonwealth Shakespeare Company, *Boston Common (p 131)*

Best **Music Deals**
★ Longy School of Music, *1 Follen St., Cambridge (p 129)*; and ★ New England Conservatory of Music, *290 Huntington Ave. (p 128)*

Best **Theater Company**
★★ Huntington Theatre Company, *264 Huntington Ave. (p 132)*

Best **Sports Venue**
★★★ Fenway Park, *4 Yawkey Way (p 131)*

Best **Holiday Event**
★★ *The Nutcracker,* Boston Ballet, *Opera House, 539 Washington St. (p 129)*

Best **Family Entertainment**
★ *Shear Madness, Charles Playhouse, 74 Warrenton St. (p 132)*

Best **First-Run Movie Theater**
★ AMC Boston Common, *175 Tremont St. (p 129)*

Best **Art House**
★ Kendall Square Cinema, *1 Kendall Sq., Cambridge (p 129)*

Best **Revival House**
★★ Brattle Theatre, *40 Brattle St., Cambridge (p 129)*

Best **Midnight Movies**
★★ Coolidge Corner Movie Theater, *290 Harvard St., Brookline (p 129)*

Fenway is the oldest ballpark in the major leagues.

Arts & Entertainment A to Z

Note: See the "Cambridge Nightlife" map (p 115) for the locations of the Cambridge establishments listed in this chapter.

Classical Music

★ **Boston Landmarks Orchestra** VARIOUS LOCATIONS The orchestra performs free (free!) concerts in historic settings—usually parks—around town on summer weekends. *Performances on Boston Common, at the Hatch Shell, and in other locations.* ☎ *617/520-2200. www.landmarksorchestra.org.*

★★ **Boston Pops** BACK BAY The Boston Symphony Orchestra's playful sibling often features celebrity guest stars. Refreshments are served at tables on the floor of Symphony Hall, and there's balcony seating without food and drink. The season runs from May to early July—ending with a week of free shows, including the Fourth of July extravaganza—plus holiday programs in December. *301 Massachusetts Ave. (Huntington Ave.)* ☎ *888/266-1200 or* ☎ *617/266-1200 (SymphonyCharge). www.bostonpops.org. Tickets $17–$74. T: Green Line E to Symphony. Map p 124.*

★★★ **Boston Symphony Orchestra** BACK BAY The BSO is one of the five best American orchestras and one of the finest in the world. The most-celebrated programs are classical music, often with a renowned guest artist or conductor. The season runs October through April. *301 Massachusetts Ave. (Huntington Ave.)* ☎ *888/266-1200 or* ☎ *617/266-1200 (SymphonyCharge). www.bso.org. Tickets $28–$108; rehearsal $17. T: Green Line E to Symphony. Map p 124.*

★★ **Emmanuel Church** BACK BAY Emmanuel's orchestra and

John Williams conducting the Boston Pops.

chorus perform Bach cantatas at Sunday services (10am) from mid-September to mid-May. *15 Newbury St. (Arlington St.)* ☎ *617/536-3356. www.emmanuelmusic.org. Free-will offering. T: Green Line to Arlington. Map p 124.*

★★ **Handel & Haydn Society** BACK BAY/FENWAY "Historically informed" concerts with period instruments and techniques might sound stodgy—until you hear the first note of a dynamic, creative performance. *Offices: 300 Massachusetts Ave.* ☎ *617/266-3605. www.handelandhaydn.org. Performing at Symphony Hall (p 128) and New England Conservatory's Jordan Hall (p 128). Map p 124.*

Concert & Performance Venues

★★★ **Hatch Shell** BACK BAY The riverside amphitheater, best known as the home of the Boston Pops' nationally televised Fourth of July concert, schedules music, dance, and other performances on

The Emmanuel Church orchestra and chorus.

most summer nights. Free Friday Flicks (family movies) begin at sunset (late Jun–late Aug). *Charles River Esplanade (off Storrow Dr.)* ☎ *617/727-5215. www.mass.gov/dcr/hatch_events.htm. Free admission. T: Red Line to Charles/MGH or Green Line to Arlington. Map p 124.*

★ **New England Conservatory's Jordan Hall** FENWAY Students and faculty performing free classical, jazz, and chamber music dominate the schedule, which includes professional artists and companies. *290 Huntington Ave. (Gainsborough St.).* ☎ *617/585-1100. www.newenglandconservatory.edu/concerts. Ticket prices vary. T: Green Line E to Symphony. Map p 124.*

★★ **Symphony Hall** BACK BAY When the BSO and the Pops are off, acoustically perfect Symphony Hall

books a wide variety of performing artists. *301 Massachusetts Ave. (Huntington Ave.)* ☎ *888/266-1200 or* ☎ *617/266-1200 (Symphony-Charge). www.bso.org. Ticket prices vary. T: Green Line E to Symphony. Map p 124.*

Concert Series

★ **Fridays at Trinity** BACK BAY Architecturally important Trinity Church features 30-minute organ recitals by local and visiting artists on Friday at 12:15pm. *206 Clarendon St. (Boylston St.).* ☎ *617/536-0944. www.trinitychurchboston.org. $5 donation suggested. T: Green Line to Copley. Map p 124.*

★★ **Isabella Stewart Gardner Museum** FENWAY The beloved museum (p 25, bullet ③) features soloists, local students, chamber

Where to Score Tickets

BosTix (☎ 617/482-2849 for information; www.artsboston.org) sells full-price and discounted advance tickets and half-price same-day tickets at its booths at Faneuil Hall Marketplace (T: Green or Blue Line to Government Center) and in Copley Square (T: Green Line to Copley). Both booths are open Tues–Sat 10am–6pm (half-price tickets go on sale at 11am) and Sun 11am–4pm. The Copley Square location is also open Mon 10am–6pm. Both booths accept cash only. The major ticket agencies that serve Boston are **Ticketmaster** (☎ 617/931-2000; www.ticketmaster.com), **Next Ticketing** (☎ 617/423-6398; www.nextticketing.com), and **Telecharge** (☎ 800/432-7250; www.telecharge.com). For information on touring Broadway shows, visit www.broadwayacrossamerica.com.

music, and jazz on weekends from late September to early May. *280 The Fenway (Museum Rd.).* ☎ *617/278-5156. www.gardnermuseum. org. Tickets (including museum admission) $20 adults, $14 seniors, $10 students, $5 kids 5–17. Kids under 5 not admitted. T: Green Line E to Museum. Map p 124.*

★ **King's Chapel Noon Hour Recitals** DOWNTOWN CROSSING Organ, instrumental, and vocal solos enliven this historic building on the Freedom Trail. Concerts are at 12:15pm on Tuesday. *58 Tremont St. (School St.).* ☎ *617/227-2155. $3 donation requested. T: Red or Green Line to Park St. Map p 124.*

★ **Longy School of Music** CAMBRIDGE   Students and faculty members from the prestigious conservatory perform at locations around the compact campus. *1 Follen St. (Garden St.). (*☎ *617/876-0956, ext. 500. www.longy.edu. Ticket prices vary; many performances free. T: Red Line to Harvard. Map p 115.*

Dance
★★ **Boston Ballet** THEATER DISTRICT   Best known for *The Nutcracker,* Boston Ballet is the fourth-largest ballet company in the country and one of the best. *Performances at the Wang Theatre (p 132) and the Opera House (p 132).* ☎ *617/695-6955 (box office) or* ☎ *800/432-7250 (Telecharge; www.telecharge. com). www.bostonballet.org. Tickets $39–$105;* Nutcracker *tickets $25–$125. T: Green Line to Boylston. Map p 124.*

Film
★ **AMC Boston Common 19** THEATER DISTRICT   The only first-run theater downtown boasts stadium seating and digital sound. It gets unbelievably crowded on weekend nights. *175 Tremont St. (Avery*

St.). ☎ *617/423-3499. www.movie watcher.com. Tickets $7–$10. T: Green Line to Boylston. Map p 124.*

★★ **Brattle Theatre** CAMBRIDGE A paragon of a revival house, the Brattle also schedules first-run independent films, talks, readings, and (remember these?) double features. *40 Brattle St. (Church St.)* ☎ *617/867-6837. www.brattlefilm.org. Tickets $7.50–$9. T: Red Line to Harvard. Map p 115.*

★★ **Coolidge Corner Movie Theater** BROOKLINE   The Coolidge Corner books independent and international films, documentaries, revivals, and midnight shows. *290 Harvard St. (Beacon St.).* ☎ *617/734-2500. www.coolidge.org. Tickets $7.50–$9.50. T: Green Line C to Coolidge Corner. Map p 124.*

★★ **Kendall Square Cinema** CAMBRIDGE   The Kendall offers alternative and foreign-language films as well as viewer-friendly raked seating and excellent concessions.

The Boston Ballet is the country's fourth-largest ballet company.

ART's production of Snow in June.

1 Kendall Sq. (Binney St.) ☎ *617/499-1996. www.landmarktheatres.com. Tickets $7–$9.25. T: Red Line to Kendall/MIT, 10-min. walk. Map p 115.*

Opera

★ **Boston Lyric Opera** THEATER DISTRICT   The area's foremost resident company performs classical and contemporary works from October through May. *Performances at the Shubert Theatre, 265 Tremont St. (Stuart St.)* ☎ *617/542-6772 or* ☎ *800/432-7250 (Telecharge). www.blo.org. Tickets $34–$166. T: Green Line to Boylston. Map p 124.*

Popular Music

★ **Agganis Arena** BOSTON UNIVERSITY   Besides booking touring rock and pop artists, the midsize venue is BU's hockey rink. *925 Commonwealth Ave. (Harry Agganis Way).* ☎ *617/353-4628 or* ☎ *617/931-2000 (Ticketmaster). www.agganisarena.com. Ticket prices vary. T: Green Line B to St. Paul St. or Pleasant St. Map p 124.*

★★ **Bank of America Pavilion** SEAPORT DISTRICT   The huge waterfront tent is a sublime summer setting for rock, pop, folk, country, rap, and jazz. *290 Northern Ave. (Congress St.)* ☎ *617/728-1600 or* ☎ *617/931-2000 (Ticketmaster). www.bankofamericapavilion.com. Ticket prices vary. T: Silver Line bus from South Station. Map p 124.*

★★ **Berklee Performance Center** BACK BAY   The Berklee College of Music is noted for its jazz and folk programs. Current students and faculty are as talented as the school's many famous alumni—and dropouts. *136 Massachusetts Ave. (Boylston St.).* ☎ *617/747-8890. www.berkleebpc.com. Ticket prices vary. T: Green Line B, C, or D to Hynes/ICA. Map p 124.*

★ **Orpheum Theatre** DOWNTOWN CROSSING   The 1852 building is rickety and cramped, but the sight lines are fantastic. *1 Hamilton Place (Tremont St.).* ☎ *617/679-0810 or* ☎ *617/931-2000 (Ticketmaster). www.teapartyconcerts.com. Ticket prices vary. T: Red or Green Line to Park St. Map p 124.*

★ **Paradise Rock Club** BOSTON UNIVERSITY   Rock and alternative artists with local, regional, and international followings play for student-intensive crowds here. *967 Commonwealth Ave. (Harry Agganis Way)* ☎ *617/562-8800 or* ☎ *617/423-6398 (Next Ticketing). www.thedise.com. Ticket prices vary. T: Green Line B to Pleasant St. Map p 124.*

★★ **Somerville Theatre** SOMERVILLE   This second-run movie theater occasionally books folk, rock, and international artists in its large main space. *55 Davis Sq. (Day St.).* ☎ *617/625-5700. www.somervilletheatreonline.com. Ticket prices vary. T: Red Line to Davis. Map p 115.*

Spectator Sports

★★★ Fenway Park FENWAY
The beloved team plays at the landmark ballpark from April to October. See p 24, bullet ➊. *4 Yawkey Way (Brookline Ave.)* ☎ *877/733-7699 for tickets. www.redsox.com. Tickets $12–$120. T: Green Line B, C, or D to Kenmore. Map p 124.*

★ TD Banknorth Garden NORTH
STATION   The city's premier arena—also known as the "Gah-din"—is home to the Celtics (NBA) and Bruins (NHL) as well as ice shows and touring rock and pop artists. *100 Legends Way (Causeway St.)* ☎ *617/624-1000. www.tdbanknorthgarden.com. Ticket prices vary. T: Green or Orange Line to North Station. Map p 124.*

Theater

★ American Repertory Theatre
CAMBRIDGE   Founded in 1980, the nationally renowned ART (say each letter) is associated with Harvard and performs at the university's Loeb Drama Center. The **Zero Arrow Theatre** (0 Arrow St., off Massachusetts Ave.) is the company's experimental space. *64 Brattle St. (Hilliard St.)* ☎ *617/547-8300.*

Commonwealth Shakespeare Company's production of Hamlet.

www.amrep.org. Tickets $10 and up. T: Red Line to Harvard. Map p 115.

★★ Blue Man Group THEATER
DISTRICT   The off-Broadway phenomenon, a trio of cobalt-colored performers backed by a rock band, enlists audience members—beware if you're sitting in the first few rows. *Charles Playhouse Stage I, 74 Warrenton St.* ☎ *617/426-6912 or* ☎ *617/931-2000 (Ticketmaster). www.blueman.com. Tickets $48 and $58. T: Green Line to Boylston. Map p 124.*

★★ Boston Center for the Arts SOUTH END   The city's top destination for contemporary theater, music, and dance, the BCA is a fun, funky leader in the local arts community. *539 Tremont St. (Clarendon St.)* ☎ *617/426-7700. www.bcaonline.org. Ticket prices vary. T: Orange Line to Back Bay. Map p 124.*

★★ Colonial Theatre THEATER
DISTRICT   This exquisite theater was built in 1900 as a legitimate stage—not a movie theater—which translates to excellent sight lines and acoustics. *106 Boylston St. (Tremont St.)* ☎ *617/426-9366. Ticket prices vary. T: Green Line to Boylston. Map p 124.*

★★ Commonwealth Shakespeare Company BOSTON COMMON   A highlight of summer is Commonwealth Shakespeare's annual production—tragedies in odd-numbered years, comedies in even-numbered years—which runs Tuesday to Sunday in July and early August. *Charles and Beacon sts.* ☎ *617/532-1252. www.freeshakespeare.org. Free admission. T: Green Line to Boylston. Map p 124.*

★★ Cutler Majestic Theatre
THEATER DISTRICT   The exquisite 1903 Beaux Arts theater books music, dance, opera, and Emerson College student productions. *219 Tremont St. (Boylston St.)*

☎ 617/824-8000 or ☎ 800/432-7250 (Telecharge). www.maj.org. Ticket prices vary. T: Green Line to Boylston. Map p 124.

★★ Huntington Theatre Company FENWAY   The leading light of Boston's professional theater scene presents contemporary works and revivals at the Boston University Theatre, with some productions at the Boston Center for the Arts (p 131). *264 Huntington Ave. (Massachusetts Ave. and Gainsborough St.)* ☎ *617/266-0800. www.huntington.org. Ticket prices vary. T: Green Line E to Symphony. Map p 124.*

★★ Opera House THEATER DISTRICT   Built as a vaudeville theater, the recently renovated Opera House is a cavernous, ornate venue that's wildly popular with touring Broadway musicals. From Thanksgiving to New Year's, Boston Ballet's *Nutcracker* takes over. *539 Washington St. (Ave. de Lafayette).* ☎ *617/880-2400. Ticket prices vary. T: Green Line to Boylston. Map p 124.*

On some Monday evenings, the Wang Theatre shows free films on an enormous screen.

★★ Sanders Theatre CAMBRIDGE   Harvard's Memorial Hall holds this three-tiered space, a student performance venue (and undergrad lecture hall) that books professional folk, classical, and world-music performers and local arts companies. *45 Quincy St. (Cambridge St.)* ☎ *617/496-2222. www.fas.harvard.edu/~memhall. Ticket prices vary. T: Red Line to Harvard. Map p 115.*

★ Shear Madness THEATER DISTRICT   The audience helps solve a murder in the course of this madcap show set in a hair salon; it's great fun and never the same twice. *Charles Playhouse Stage II (downstairs), 74 Warrenton St.* ☎ *617/426-5225. www.shearmadness.com. Tickets $40. T: Green Line to Boylston. Map p 124.*

★ Shubert Theatre THEATER DISTRICT   The Shubert stages varied musical performances (including opera) and books touring Broadway shows. *265 Tremont St. (Stuart St.)* ☎ *617/482-9393. www.wangcenter.org. Ticket prices vary. T: Green Line to Boylston. Map p 124.*

★ Wang Theatre THEATER DISTRICT   One of the largest stages in Boston was built as a movie theater and has some of the worst sight lines in town from the upper balconies. Seats on the first two levels are worth the price—especially if you're here for dance. *270 Tremont St. (Stuart St.)* ☎ *617/482-9393. www.wangcenter.org. Ticket prices vary. T: Green Line to Boylston. Map p 124.*

★★ Wilbur Theatre THEATER DISTRICT   The Wilbur is a jewel box of a theater, the smallest local stage to handle Broadway previews and touring companies. *246 Tremont St. (Stuart St.)* ☎ *617/423-4008. Ticket prices vary. T: Green Line to Boylston. Map p 124.* ●

Lodging **Best Bets**

Best **in Boston**
★★★ Boston Harbor Hotel $$$$ *Rowes Wharf* (p 138)

Best **in Cambridge**
★★★ The Charles Hotel $$$$ *1 Bennett St.* (p 139)

Best **Views**
★★★ Westin Copley Place Boston $$$ *10 Huntington Ave.* (p 146)

Most **Romantic**
★★ Eliot Hotel $$$$ *370 Commonwealth Ave.* (p 140)

Best **for Business**
★★★ Langham Boston Hotel $$$ *250 Franklin St.* (p 143)

Best **for Families**
★★ Doubletree Guest Suites $$–$$$ *400 Soldiers Field Rd.* (p 140)

Best **Place to See Celebrities**
★★★ Four Seasons Hotel $$$$ *200 Boylston St.* (p 141)

Best **Historic Hotel**
★★ The Fairmont Copley Plaza Hotel $$$$ *138 St. James Ave.* (p 140)

Best **Boutique Hotel**
★★ Fifteen Beacon $$$$ *15 Beacon St.* (p 141)

Most **Hospitable to Motorists**
★ MidTown Hotel $$ *220 Huntington Ave.* (p 144)

Best **Pool**
★★ Sheraton Boston Hotel $$$$ *39 Dalton St.* (p 146)

Best **Deal on Newbury Street**
★ Newbury Guest House $$ *261 Newbury St.* (p 144)

Best **Access to the River**
★★★ Royal Sonesta Hotel $$$ *5 Cambridge Pkwy., Cambridge* (p 146)

Best **Design**
★ Bulfinch Hotel $$ *107 Merrimac St.* (p 139)

Best **for Marathon Fanatics**
★ Charlesmark Hotel $$ *655 Boylston St.* (p 139)

Best **for Red Sox Fanatics**
★★ Hotel Commonwealth $$$$ *500 Commonwealth Ave.* (p 142)

Best **for Celtics and Bruins Fanatics**
★★★ Onyx Hotel $$$ *155 Portland St.* (p 145)

If I were traveling with someone else's credit cards, I'd head straight to the Four Seasons.

Cambridge **Lodging**

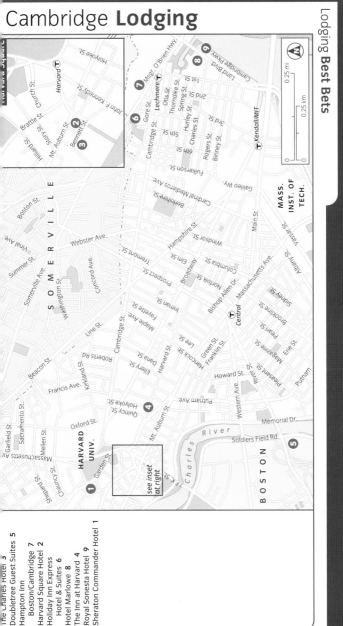

The Charles Hotel **3**
Doubletree Guest Suites **5**
Hampton Inn
  Boston/Cambridge **7**
Harvard Square Hotel **2**
Holiday Inn Express
  Hotel & Suites **6**
Hotel Marlowe **8**
The Inn at Harvard **4**
Royal Sonesta Hotel **9**
Sheraton Commander Hotel **1**

Boston **Lodging**

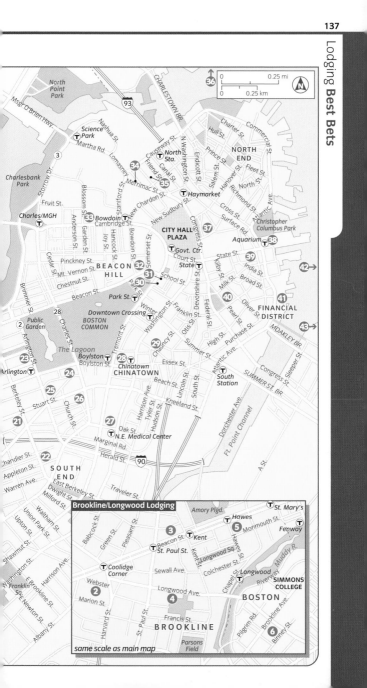

North Point Park

Msgr O'Brien Hwy

Science Park ⓣ

North Sta. ⓣ

NORTH END

Charlesbank Park

Storrow Dr.

Martha Rd.

Nashua St.

Lomasney

Charles/MGH ⓣ

Fruit St.

Blossom St.

Cambridge St.

Bowdoin ⓣ ㉝

New Chardon St.

Haymarket ⓣ

Cross St.

Christopher Columbus Park

Anderson St.

Garden St.

Joy St.

Hancock

Bowdoin St.

Somerset St.

CITY HALL PLAZA

Aquarium ⓣ ㊳

Cedar St.

Pinckney St.

BEACON HILL ㉜

Govt. Ctr. ⓣ

Court St.

State St. ㊴

India St.

State ⓣ

Kilby St.

Broad St.

㊷

Mt. Vernon St.

Chestnut St.

㉛

㉚

School St.

Devonshire St.

Milk St.

Oliver St.

FINANCIAL DISTRICT ㊶

Beacon St.

Park St. ⓣ

Winter St.

Franklin St.

Federal St.

Pearl St.

MOAKLEY BR

㊸

Public Garden

㉘

Charles St.

Downtown Crossing

BOSTON COMMON

Washington St.

Otis St.

High St.

Purchase St.

Summer St.

Congress St.

Sleeper St.

Arlington ⓣ

The Lagoon

Boylston ⓣ

Boylston St. ㉘

Tremont St.

㉙

Chauncy St.

Summer St.

Atlantic Ave.

South Station ⓣ

SUMMER ST. BR

㉓

㉔

Chinatown CHINATOWN

Essex St.

Beach St.

Lincoln St.

South St.

Kneeland St.

Dorchester Ave.

Ft. Point Channel

Berkeley St.

㉑

㉕

㉖

Stuart St.

Church St.

Harrison Ave.

Tyler St.

Hudson St.

A St.

Chandler St.

㉒

㉗

Oak St.

N.E. Medical Center ⓣ

Marginal Rd.

Appleton St.

SOUTH END

East Berkeley St.

Herald St.

Warren Ave.

Dwight St.

Milford St.

Traveler St.

Waltham St.

Union Park St.

Upton St.

Shawmut Ave.

Washington St.

E Brookline St.

Harrison Ave.

Franklin Sq.

SE Newton St.

Albany St.

Brookline/Longwood Lodging

Amory Plgd.

St. Mary's ⓣ

Hawes ⓣ

❸

Kent ⓣ

Monmouth St.

❺

Fenway ⓣ

Babcock St.

Green St.

Pleasant St.

Beacon St. ⓣ

St. Paul St. ⓣ

Longwood Sq.

Hawes St.

Colchester St.

Coolidge Corner ⓣ

Sewall Ave.

Chapel St.

Longwood ⓣ

Riverway

Muddy R.

SIMMONS COLLEGE

Webster ❷

Longwood Ave.

BOSTON

Marion St.

❹

Brookline Ave.

Harvard St.

St. Paul St.

Francis St.

❻

Birney St.

Pilgrim Rd.

BROOKLINE

Parsons Field

same scale as main map

0.25 mi
0.25 km

Lodging **A to Z**

Anthony's Town House OUT-SKIRTS/BROOKLINE   The good-size rooms at this homey guesthouse share bathrooms and have high-speed Internet access. The four-story 19th-century brownstone boasts high ceilings and ornate Queen Anne or Victorian interiors. *1085 Beacon St. (Hawes and Carlton sts.), Brookline* ☎ *617/566-3972. www.anthonystownhouse.com. 10 units. Doubles $68–$98. No credit cards. T: Green Line C to Hawes St. Map p 136.*

★★ kids Best Western Boston/ The Inn at Longwood Medical FENWAY   This modern hotel in the heart of the Longwood Medical area is convenient to the Fenway area. Rooms are quite large and suites have kitchen facilities. *342 Longwood Ave. (Brookline Ave.)* ☎ *800/ 468-2378. www.innatlongwood.com. 161 units. Doubles $139–$259. AE, DC, DISC, MC, V. T: Green Line D or E to Longwood. Map p 136.*

★★★ Boston Harbor Hotel WATERFRONT   The most luxurious hotel in town boasts gorgeous rooms with marble bathrooms and mahogany furnishings, great views,

grand public spaces with museum-quality art on display, and plentiful amenities. *Rowes Wharf (Atlantic and Northern aves.)* ☎ *800/752-7077. www.bhh.com. 230 units. Doubles $295–$595. AE, DC, DISC, MC, V. T: Blue Line to Aquarium or Red Line to South Station. Map p 136.*

★ kids Boston Marriott Copley Place BACK BAY   A fine hotel for business or pleasure, with perks (including a pool) for both. The generously sized, recently refurbished rooms boast Queen Anne–style mahogany furnishings. *110 Huntington Ave. (Dartmouth St.)* ☎ *800/ 228-9290. www.copleymarriott.com. 1,147 units. Doubles $159–$329. AE, DC, DISC, MC, V. T: Orange Line to Back Bay or Green Line to Copley. Map p 136.*

★★ kids Boston Marriott Long Wharf WATERFRONT   The great location and views outshine the pleasant accommodations (large, sunny rooms) and good business features. *296 State St. (Atlantic Ave.)* ☎ *800/228-9290. www.marriott longwharf.com. 400 units. Doubles $159–$450. AE, DC, DISC, MC, V. T: Blue Line to Aquarium. Map p 136.*

The Boston Harbor Hotel's landmark arch has become a symbol of Boston.

Just off Harvard Square, the Charles is the finest hotel in Cambridge.

Boston Park Plaza Hotel & Towers BACK BAY   A magnet for conventions, meetings, and functions, the Park Plaza also books many tour groups. Built in 1927, the hotel offers modern comforts but maintains an old-fashioned feel. *64 Arlington St. (Providence and Stuart sts.)* ☎ *800/225-2008. www.boston parkplaza.com. 950 units. Doubles $139–$299. AE, DC, DISC, MC, V. T: Green Line to Arlington. Map p 136.*

★ **Brookline Courtyard by Marriott** OUTSKIRTS/BROOKLINE Boston is 15 minutes from this business hotel in a fun neighborhood. Rooms are large but generic—suburban style in an urban setting. *40 Webster St. (Beacon and Harvard sts.), Brookline.* ☎ *866/296-2296. www.brooklinecourtyard.com. 188 units. Doubles $159–$309. AE, DC, DISC, MC, V. T: Green Line C to Coolidge Corner. Map p 136.*

★ **Bulfinch Hotel** NORTH STATION   This triangular building's smallish, custom-outfitted rooms are a great deal for the price. The 1904 building's many unique architectural details enhance the "budget boutique" feel. *107 Merrimac St. (Lancaster St.)* ☎ *800/424-6423. www.bulfinchhotel.com. 80 units.*

Doubles $169–$324. AE, DC, DISC, MC, V. T: Green or Orange Line to North Station. Map p 136.

★ **Chandler Inn Hotel** SOUTH END   Small but comfortable rooms in a convenient location help the largest gay-owned property in town sell out regularly. *26 Chandler St. (Berkeley St.)* ☎ *800/842-3450. www.chandlerinn.com. 56 units. Doubles $129–$169. AE, DC, DISC, MC, V. T: Orange Line to Back Bay. Map p 136.*

★★★ **kids The Charles Hotel** CAMBRIDGE   The top-notch accommodations, service, restaurants, health club, and spa make the Charles Cambridge's finest hotel. The good-size rooms are deceptively simple; their unfussy Shaker style contrasts with pampering details like quilts, down comforters, and a TV in the bathroom. *1 Bennett St. (Eliot St.), Cambridge.* ☎ *800/ 882-1818. www.charleshotel.com. 293 units. Doubles $259–$599. AE, DC, MC, V. T: Red Line to Harvard. Map p 135.*

★ **Charlesmark Hotel** BACK BAY Sleek contemporary design makes the compact rooms (many overlooking the Marathon finish line) feel huge. Custom furnishings give the

The rooftop pool is one of the distinctive features of the Colonnade Hotel Boston.

hotel a boutique feel. *655 Boylston St. (Dartmouth and Exeter sts.)* ☎ *617/247-1212. www.the charlesmark.com. 33 units. Doubles $99–$249 w/breakfast. AE, DC, DISC, MC, V. T: Green Line to Copley. Map p 136.*

★★ **kids** **Colonnade Hotel Boston** BACK BAY   The elegance of the Colonnade's quiet, high-ceilinged public spaces carries over to the large, contemporary guest rooms. Young travelers will enjoy the rooftop pool and VIKids program. Excellent service. *120 Huntington Ave. (W. Newton and Garrison sts.)* ☎ *800/962-3030. www.colonnade hotel.com. 285 units. Doubles $175–$425. AE, DC, DISC, MC, V. T: Green Line E to Prudential. Map p 136.*

Copley Square Hotel BACK BAY The old-fashioned atmosphere distinguishes this small hotel with decent-size rooms from its convention-oriented neighbors. *47 Huntington Ave. (Exeter St.)* ☎ *800/225-7062. www.copleysquarehotel.com. 143 units. Doubles $139–$295. AE, DC, DISC, MC, V. T: Green Line to Copley. Map p 136.*

★★ **kids** **Doubletree Guest Suites** OUTSKIRTS/BROOKLINE Each sizable two-room suite has a

fridge; the T isn't nearby, but this is a deal if you're driving. *400 Soldiers Field Rd. (at Mass. Pike Brighton/ Cambridge exit)* ☎ *800/222-8733. www.doubletree.com. 308 units. Doubles $129–$309. AE, DC, DISC, MC, V. Map p 135.*

★★ **kids** **Doubletree Hotel Boston Downtown** CHINATOWN The modern, centrally located Doubletree gives guests access to a huge YMCA. Rooms are compact but the location is great. *821 Washington St. (Kneeland and Oak sts.)* ☎ *800/222-8733. http://doubletree. hilton.com. 267 units. Doubles $129–$299. AE, DC, DISC, MC, V. T: Orange Line to New England Medical Center. Map p 136.*

★★★ **Eliot Hotel** BACK BAY Most units are large, romantic suites with antique furnishings, giving the Eliot a residential feel; the accommodating staff completes the illusion. *370 Commonwealth Ave. (Mass Ave.)* ☎ *800/443-5468. www.eliot hotel.com. 95 units. Doubles $255–$435. AE, DC, MC, V. T: Green Line B, C, or D to Hynes/ICA. Map p 136.*

★★ **The Fairmont Copley Plaza Hotel** BACK BAY   Ornate decor and courtly service make this hotel, built in 1912, a Boston classic.

Posh fabrics and custom furnishings will make you feel right at home—especially if your home is a mansion. *138 St. James Ave. (Dartmouth and Clarendon sts.)* ☎ *800/257-7544. www.fairmont.com/copley-plaza. 383 units. Doubles from $259. AE, DC, MC, V. T: Green Line to Copley or Orange Line to Back Bay. Map p 136.*

★★ **Fifteen Beacon** BEACON HILL Over-the-top luxury and contemporary style are the hallmarks of the city's premier boutique property. Management bends over backward to keep demanding guests happy. *15 Beacon St. (Bowdoin and Somerset sts.)* ☎ *877/982-3226. www.xvbeacon.com. 60 units. Doubles from $395. AE, DC, DISC, MC, V. T: Red or Green Line to Park St. Map p 136.*

★★★ **Four Seasons Hotel** BACK BAY The best hotel in New England offers its pampered guests everything they could ever want—for a price. *200 Boylston St. (Arlington St.)* ☎ *800/819-5053. www.fourseasons.com/boston. 272 units. Doubles $425–$650. AE, DC, DISC, MC, V. T: Green Line to Arlington. Map p 136.*

★ kids **Hampton Inn Boston/ Cambridge** CAMBRIDGE This hotel has been a business-traveler favorite since opening in 2002. The cookie-cutter rooms offer no surprises—they're generic but quite comfortable. *191 Msgr. O'Brien Hwy. (Water St.), Cambridge.* ☎ *800/426-7866. www.bostoncambridge. hamptoninn.com. 114 units. Doubles $129–$304 w/breakfast. AE, DC, DISC, MC, V. T: Green Line to Lechmere. Map p 135.*

★ **Harborside Inn** WATERFRONT A renovated 19th-century warehouse across the street from Faneuil Hall Marketplace, this hotel represents excellent value. Rooms are outfitted with hardwood floors, Oriental rugs, and Victorian-style furniture. *185 State St. (Atlantic Ave.)* ☎ *888/723-7565. www.harborside innboston.com. 54 units. Doubles $120–$210. AE, DC, DISC, MC, V. T: Blue Line to Aquarium. Map p 136.*

★ **Harvard Square Hotel** CAMBRIDGE You're paying for the fantastic location, not the well-maintained but utilitarian accommodations here. *110 Mount Auburn St. (Eliot St.)* ☎ *800/458-5886.*

The Eliot Hotel is next door to the equally elegant Harvard Club.

The Fairmont Copley Plaza—the "grande dame" of Boston.

www.harvardsquarehotel.com. 73 units. Doubles $99–$269. AE, DC, DISC, MC, V. T: Red Line to Harvard. Map p 135.

★★ Hilton Boston Back Bay
BACK BAY   The 26-story business hotel, with large rooms featuring oversized work desks, also accommodates families and offers great views from the upper floors. *40 Dalton St. (Scotia and Boylston sts.)* ☎ 800/874-0663. www.hilton.com. 385 units. Doubles $149–$399. AE, DC, DISC, MC, V. T: Green Line B, C, or D to Hynes/ICA. Map p 136.

★ Hilton Boston Logan Airport AIRPORT   An excellent business choice, the Hilton is a good fallback for vacationers priced out of downtown. *1 Hotel Dr. (Terminal Rd.)* ☎ 800/445-8667. www.hilton.com. 599 units. Doubles $99–$399. AE, DC, DISC, MC, V. T: Blue Line to Airport, shuttle bus. Map p 136.

★ kids Holiday Inn Boston Brookline OUTSKIRTS/BROOKLINE The trade-off for the commute to downtown is a pleasant hotel with large, well-maintained rooms and a small pool. *1200 Beacon St. (St. Paul St.)* ☎ 800/465-4329. www.bos-brookline.holiday-inn.com. 225 units. Doubles $149–$229. AE, MC, V. T:

Green Line C to St. Paul St. Map p 136.

★ Holiday Inn Express Hotel & Suites CAMBRIDGE   Weigh the price and location against the limited services and amenities; this is a solid choice. *250 Msgr. O'Brien Hwy. (3rd St.)* ☎ 888/887-7690. www.hiexpress.com. 112 units. Doubles $109–$199 w/breakfast. AE, DC, DISC, MC, V. T: Green Line to Lechmere. Map p 135.

★ Holiday Inn Select Boston Government Center BEACON HILL   Adjacent to Mass. General Hospital, this is a well-equipped business hotel. *5 Blossom St. (Cambridge St.)* ☎ 888/465-4329. www.hiselect.com/bos-government. 303 units. Doubles $130–$259. AE, DC, DISC, MC, V. T: Red Line to Charles/MGH. Map p 136.

★★★ Hotel Commonwealth
BACK BAY   The lavishly appointed guest rooms (Italian linens, marble bathrooms) overlook Kenmore Square or (across the Mass. Pike) Fenway Park. It was opened in a brand-new building in 2003 but has a very traditional look and feel. *500 Commonwealth Ave. (Kenmore St.)* ☎ 866/784-4000. www.hotelcommonwealth.com. 150 units.

Doubles $209–$349. AE, DC, DISC, MC, V. T: Green Line B, C, or D to Kenmore. Map p 136.

★★ kids **Hotel Marlowe** CAMBRIDGE   This posh yet funky business hotel has a family-friendly vibe. Good-sized rooms are elegantly decorated, with fun touches like leopard-print carpet. *25 Land Blvd. (Msgr. O'Brien Hwy.)* ☎ *800/825-7040. www.hotelmarlowe.com. 236 units. Doubles $189–$399. AE, DC, DISC, MC, V. T: Green Line to Lechmere or Red Line to Kendall. Map p 135.*

★ **Hotel 140** BACK BAY   Small rooms (some with one twin bed) on three floors of a newly renovated former YMCA. But just look at those rates. *140 Clarendon St. (Stuart St.)* ☎ *800/714-0140. www.hotel140. com. 40 units. Doubles $129–$179 w/breakfast. AE, MC, V. T: Orange Line to Back Bay. Map p 136.*

★★ kids **Hyatt Regency Boston Financial District** DOWNTOWN CROSSING   The business-oriented Hyatt slashes weekend prices. Spacious rooms feature luxurious European-style appointments. *1 Ave. de Lafayette (Washington St.)* ☎ *800/233-1234. www. hyattregencyboston.com. 500 units. Doubles $189–$375. AE, DC, DISC, MC, V. T: Red or Orange Line to Downtown Crossing. Map p 136.*

★★ kids **The Inn at Harvard** CAMBRIDGE   A retreat from the hubbub of Harvard Square, this hotel boasts excellent business amenities. Elegant rooms feature original paintings on loan from the Fogg museum. *1201 Massachusetts Ave. (Quincy St.)* ☎ *800/458-5886. www.theinnatharvard.com. 113 units. Doubles $149–$359. AE, DC, DISC, MC, V. T: Red Line to Harvard. Map p 135.*

★★ **Jurys Boston Hotel** BACK BAY   Plush lodgings in the former police headquarters helped this Irish chain make a splash in the Boston market. *350 Stuart St. (Berkeley St.)* ☎ *866/534-6835. www.jurys doyle.com. 225 units. Doubles $155–$435. AE, DC, DISC, MC, V. T: Orange Line to Back Bay. Map p 136.*

★★ **Langham Boston Hotel** FINANCIAL DISTRICT   The city's top business hotel, in an unbeatable location, does a lot of weekend leisure business. *250 Franklin St. (Post Office Sq.)* ☎ *800/791-7794. www.langhamhotels.com. 325 units. Doubles $159–$475. AE, DC, DISC, MC, V. T: Blue or Orange Line to State. Map p 136.*

★★ **The Lenox Hotel** BACK BAY   A turn-of-the-20th-century hotel with 21st-century features, the Lenox is a good alternative to this

The newly renovated Hotel 140 offers cozy rooms at bargain (for Boston) prices.

The sleek atmosphere of the Nine Zero hotel is a welcome departure for Boston.

neighborhood's behemoths. Spacious, high-ceilinged rooms feature custom furniture. Excellent views from the top two floors. *61 Exeter St. (Boylston St.)* ☎ *800/225-7676. www.lenoxhotel.com. 212 units. Doubles $179–$329. AE, DC, DISC, MC, V. T: Green Line to Copley. Map p 136.*

★ **kids** **Longwood Inn** OUTSKIRTS/BROOKLINE This sprawling Victorian guesthouse backs up to a large playground. Most of the comfy-cozy rooms have private bathrooms. *123 Longwood Ave. (Marshall St.)* ☎ *617/566-8615. www.longwood-inn.com. 22 units. Doubles $69–$129. AE, DISC, MC, V. T: Green Line D to Longwood. Map p 136.*

★★ **kids** **Marriott Residence Inn Boston Harbor**
CHARLESTOWN This all-suite hotel on the water is a good alternative to downtown. Many of the generously sized rooms have harbor views. *34–44 Charles River Ave. (Chelsea St.)* ☎ *866/296-2297. www.marriott. com/bostw. 168 units. Doubles $169–$359 w/breakfast. AE, DC, DISC, MC, V. T: Orange Line to Community College. Map p 136.*

★ **kids** **The MidTown Hotel**
BACK BAY This motel-like hotel has large rooms, small bathrooms, a seasonal outdoor pool, and, best of all, free parking. *220 Huntington Ave. (Massachusetts Ave. and Cumberland St.)* ☎ *800/343-1177. www. midtownhotel.com. 159 units. Doubles $119–$259. AE, DC, DISC, MC, V. T: Green Line E to Symphony. Map p 136.*

★★ **Millennium Bostonian Hotel** FANEUIL HALL MARKETPLACE Three renovated 19th-century buildings hold this unexpectedly elegant business hotel. Rooms vary in size and style, but all feature top-of-the-line furnishings and amenities. *26 North St. (Clinton St.)* ☎ *800/343-0922. www.millennium hotels.com. 201 units. Doubles $149–$329. AE, DC, DISC, MC, V. T: Green or Orange Line to Haymarket. Map p 136.*

★ **Newbury Guest House** BACK BAY This sophisticated inn, housed in a pair of converted 1880s town houses, offers comfortable accommodations at modest rates. Reserve early. *261 Newbury St. (Fairfield and Gloucester sts.)* ☎ *800/437-7668. www.newburyguesthouse.com. 32* units. Doubles $140–$195 w/breakfast. AE, DC, DISC, MC, V. T: Green Line B, C, or D to Hynes/ICA. Map p 136.

★★ **Nine Zero** DOWNTOWN CROSSING The contemporary style feels better suited to SoHo or South Beach, but this luxurious hotel makes it work. 90 Tremont St. (Bromfield St.) ☎ 866/646-3937. www.ninezerohotel.com. 189 units. Doubles $289–$500. AE, DC, DISC, MC, V. T: Red or Green Line to Park St. Map p 136.

★ **kids Omni Parker House** DOWNTOWN CROSSING In business since 1855, the Parker House offers a wide range of rooms, from compact to dazzling. Units aren't huge, but nicely appointed and well maintained. 60 School St. (Tremont St.) ☎ 800/843-6664. www.omni hotels.com. 551 units. Doubles $189–$289. AE, DC, DISC, MC, V. T: Green or Blue Line to Government Center. Map p 136.

★★ **Onyx Hotel** NORTH STATION The hotel's contemporary jewel-toned boutique decor contrasts with the business amenities and gentrifying neighborhood. 155 Portland St. (Causeway St.) ☎ 866/660-6699. www.onyxhotel.com. 112 units. Doubles $209–$329. AE, DC,

Parker House rolls and Boston cream pie were invented at the Omni Parker House.

DISC, MC, V. T: Green or Orange Line to North Station. Map p 136.

★ **kids Radisson Hotel Boston** THEATER DISTRICT Large guest rooms, great views, and private balconies help make up for the Radisson's less-than-scenic neighborhood. 200 Stuart St. (Charles St. S.) ☎ 800/333-3333. www.radisson.com/bostonma. 356 units. Doubles $159–$369. AE, DC, DISC, MC, V. T: Green Line to Boylston. Map p 136.

★★ **The Ritz-Carlton, Boston** BACK BAY The traditional Boston hotel is famous for its luxe accommodations, great location, and courteous staff. 15 Arlington St. (Newbury St.) ☎ 800/241-3333. www. ritzcarlton.com. 273 units. Doubles

The Onyx Hotel has a custom-designed (by her mom) Britney Spears room.

The Royal Sonesta hugs the riverbank, offering walkers and joggers easy access.

from $295. AE, DC, DISC, MC, V. T: Green Line to Arlington. Map p 136.

★★ The Ritz-Carlton, Boston Common THEATER DISTRICT The 21st-century version of the classic original is just as luxurious but ultra-modern, with a great health club. *10 Avery St. (Tremont and Washington sts.)* ☎ *800/241-3333. www.ritz carlton.com. 193 units. Doubles from $295. AE, DC, DISC, MC, V. T: Green Line to Boylston. Map p 136.*

★★ kids Royal Sonesta Hotel CAMBRIDGE This luxurious, tech-savvy hotel offers easy access to MIT, the Museum of Science, Boston, and the river. The spacious, modern rooms offer lovely river and city views. *5 Cambridge Pkwy. (CambridgeSide Place)* ☎ *800/766-3782. www.sonesta.com/boston. 400 units. Doubles $239–$319. AE, DC, DISC, MC, V. T: Green Line to Lechmere. Map p 135.*

★★ kids Seaport Hotel SOUTH BOSTON The kid-friendly staff and pool, and the proximity to the Children's Museum make the Seaport popular with families. *1 Seaport Lane (Northern Ave.)* ☎ *877/732-7678. www.seaportboston.com. 426 units. Doubles $189–$299. AE, DC, DISC, MC, V. T: Red Line to South Station, Silver Line bus. Map p 136.*

★★ kids Sheraton Boston Hotel BACK BAY This huge, well-appointed hotel has something for everyone. The large, contemporary rooms offer gorgeous views from the higher floors. *39 Dalton St. (Belvidere St.)* ☎ *800/325-3535. www.sheraton.com/boston. 1,215 units. Doubles $129–$409. AE, DC, DISC, MC, V. T: Green Line E to Prudential. Map p 136.*

★ Sheraton Commander Hotel CAMBRIDGE Traditional in every detail, from the colonial-style decor to the helpful service, this hotel is a Cambridge classic. *16 Garden St. (Berkeley St.)* ☎ *800/325-3535. www.sheratoncommander.com. 175 units. Doubles $109–$385. AE, DC, DISC, MC, V. T: Red Line to Harvard. Map p 135.*

★★ kids The Westin Copley Place Boston BACK BAY The views are so good (the best in town) that the spacious rooms and business amenities are almost an afterthought. *10 Huntington Ave. (Dartmouth St.)* ☎ *800/937-8461. www.westin.com/copleyplace. 803 units. Doubles $179–$479. AE, DC, DISC, MC, V. T: Green Line to Copley. Map p 136.* ●

10 The Best Day Trips & Excursions

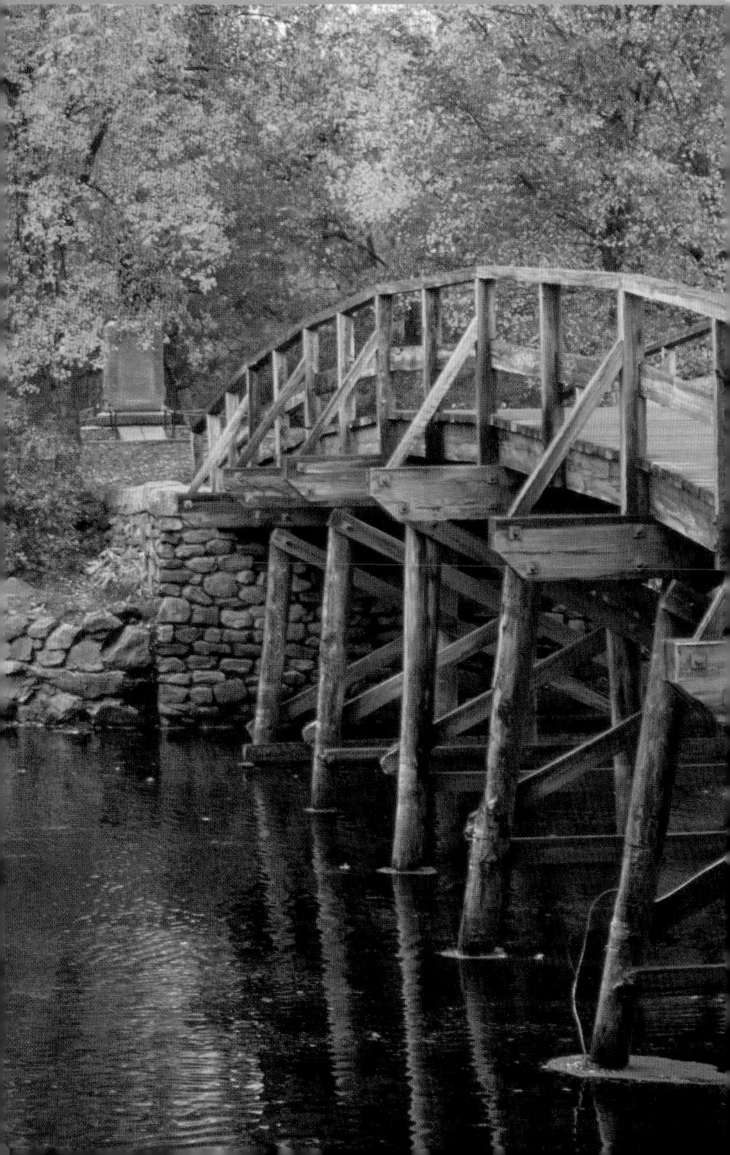

Concord

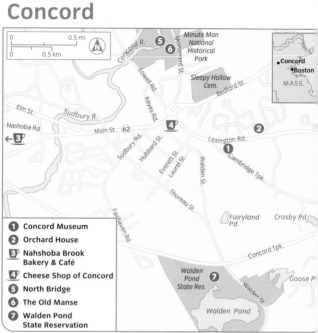

- **1** Concord Museum
- **2** Orchard House
- **3** Nahshoba Brook Bakery & Café
- **4** Cheese Shop of Concord
- **5** North Bridge
- **6** The Old Manse
- **7** Walden Pond State Reservation

Over the course of three-plus centuries, Concord (say "conquered") has grown from a country village to a prosperous suburb of about 16,000. The first official battle of the Revolutionary War took place at the North Bridge on April 19, 1775. By the mid–19th century, an impressive constellation of literary stars—Ralph Waldo Emerson, Henry Wadsworth Longfellow, Henry David Thoreau, and Louisa May Alcott—called the town home. Present-day Concord preserves and honors that rich history. START: **Jump in the car and follow Route 2 from Cambridge until you see signs for Lincoln; where the road takes a sharp left, go straight, following signs for HISTORIC CONCORD. If it's not rush hour, the trip from Boston takes 30 to 40 minutes.**

1 ★★ kids **Concord Museum.** This museum tells the story of the town in informative exhibits that incorporate intriguing artifacts, murals, films, maps, and documents. A one-time Native American settlement, Concord is perhaps best known as a Revolutionary War battleground. In the 19th century, it

was a literary and intellectual center with a thriving clock-making industry. The town was also an important player in the 20th-century historic preservation movement. Many museum displays focus on the big names: You'll see one of the lanterns immortalized by Longfellow in "Paul Revere's Ride" ("one if by land, two if by sea"), the contents of Emerson's study, and a large collection of Thoreau's belongings. The period furniture, silver, clocks, and (my favorites) embroidery samplers offer an engaging look at the lives of regular people. If you're traveling with kids, be sure to pick up a family activity pack, which has some fun hands-on components. ⏱ *1–1½ hrs. Cambridge Turnpike at Lexington Rd.* ☎ *978/369-9609 (recorded info) or* ☎ *978/369-9763. www.concordmuseum.org. Admission $8 adults, $7 seniors and students, $5 kids 6–17, free for kids under 6. June–Aug daily 9am–5pm; Apr–May & Sept–Dec Mon–Sat 9am–5pm, Sun noon–5pm; Jan–Mar Mon–Sat 11am–4pm, Sun 1–4pm.*

2 ★★★ kids **Orchard House.** Louisa May Alcott lives! Not really, but the author did live here, where she wrote and set her beloved novel *Little Women* (1868). Louisa and her sisters—the models for *Little Women*'s March family—come to life on the guided tour, the only way to see the house. Numerous heirlooms survive; I especially like Louisa's little desk and the miniature pieces of furniture that appear to be from a dollhouse (they're actually a traveling salesman's samples). Louisa's father bought this land in 1857, and the family lived here from 1858 to 1877. Check ahead for information on the extensive schedule of special events and holiday programs. ⏱ *1 hr. On autumn Saturdays, try to arrive before noon. 399 Lexington Rd.* ☎ *978/369-4118. www.louisamayalcott.org. Guided tours $8 adults, $7 seniors and students, $5 kids 6–17, free for kids under 6, $20 families. Apr–Oct Mon–Sat 10am–4:30pm, Sun 1–4:30pm; Nov–Mar Mon–Fri 11am–2:45pm, Sat 10am–4:30pm, Sun 1–4:30pm. Closed Jan 1–15.*

3 Now it's picnic time. My top choice is in West Concord: **Nashoba Brook Bakery & Café** (152 Commonwealth Ave.; ☎ 978/318-1999; $), which makes its own bread, pastries, soups, salads, and sandwiches. In downtown Concord, the **4** **Cheese Shop of Concord** (25–31 Walden St.; ☎ 978/369-5778; $), sells sandwiches, soups, and all the trimmings, including chocolates. While you're laying in provisions, stash away a snack for later, when I'll be sending you to Walden Pond, which doesn't have a food concession. Tote your treats to Monument Square or proceed to the North Bridge, our next stop.

5 ★ kids **North Bridge.** Off Monument Street outside Concord

Orchard House, the setting of Little Women.

Center, a path leads to North Bridge, a reproduction of the wooden structure that spanned the Concord River in April 1775, when the Revolutionary War began. Tune out the chatter of visitors and the hum of engines, and you can almost imagine the battle commemorated in Ralph Waldo Emerson's poem "Concord Hymn," the first stanza of which is engraved on the base of the *Minute Man* statue near the bridge. Daniel Chester French, the sculptor of the John Harvard Statue in Cambridge and the seated Abraham Lincoln at the president's memorial in Washington D.C., created the iconic image of the militiaman with a musket in one hand and a plow handle in the other. A plaque on the other side of the bridge honors the British soldiers who died in the battle. Up the hill in the National Park Service visitor center, a diorama and video program illustrate the battle, and rangers are on duty if you have questions. To get there, you can walk across the grounds or jump back in the car for the 2-minute ride. ⏲ *45 min. Minute Man National Historical Park, North Bridge Visitor Center, 174 Liberty St. (off Monument St.)* ☎ *978/369-6993. www.nps.gov/mima. Free admission. Daily 9am–5pm (until 4pm in winter).*

❻ ★ The Old Manse. A longtime family home, the Old Manse figures almost accidentally in an important part of the town's literary history. The Reverend William Emerson built the Old Manse in 1770, and his grandson Ralph Waldo Emerson later worked on the essay "Nature" in the study. Newlywed Nathaniel Hawthorne moved here in 1842; he looks forbidding and serious in most of his portraits, but on the enlightening guided tour of the Old Manse (the only way to see the interior), you'll meet a light-hearted Hawthorne who collaborated with

Rev. William Emerson watched the Battle of Concord from the yard of the Old Manse.

his new bride, Sophia Peabody, to scratch messages with her diamond ring on two windows. Henry David Thoreau planted a vegetable garden as a wedding present, and a re-creation of that project is on the grounds today. The Old Manse wasn't the permanent home of any of the town's big names; you've already seen Louisa May Alcott's, and if you're interested in visiting Emerson's or Hawthorne's, ask at the chamber of commerce office or visit the chamber website for information. ⏲ *1 hr. 269 Monument St. (at North Bridge).* ☎ *978/369-3909. www.oldmanse.org. Guided tour $8 adults, $7 seniors and students, $5 kids 6–12, free for kids under 6, $25 families. Mid-Apr to Oct Mon–Sat 10am–5pm, Sun and holidays noon–5pm (last tour at 4:30pm). Closed Nov to mid-Apr.*

❼ ★★ kids Walden Pond State Reservation. On the way back to Boston, stop off at one of the most famous places in New England. Walden Pond was home to eccentric author Henry David Thoreau for 2 years, 2 months, and 2 days in the mid-1840s, and if not

Concord: **Practical Matters**

Driving is the most efficient way to get to and around Concord. You can also take the **MBTA** commuter rail (☎ 800/392-6100 or ☎ 617/222-3200; www.mbta.com) from Boston's North Station or Cambridge's Porter Square. Check the schedule well in advance—outbound service is limited, especially on weekends. The **Chamber of Commerce,** 15 Walden St., Suite 7 (☎ 978/369-3120; www.concordchamberofcommerce.org), maintains a visitor center at 58 Main St., 1 block south of Monument Square. It's open daily 9:30am–4:30pm from April through October; public restrooms in the same building are open year-round. The chamber office is open year-round Monday through Friday; hours vary, so call ahead.

for that association, the area around the pond would likely have become valuable residential real estate many years ago. Instead, the legacy of the founder of the conservation movement is a gorgeous, surprisingly unspoiled state park property that allows hiking, swimming, fishing, and other low-impact activities but not dogs or bikes. ⏱ *1 hr. Arrive early or late in the day in the summer and fall, when the rangers close the park to newcomers after it reaches capacity (1,000). 915 Walden St. (Rte. 126), off Route 2.* ☎ *978/369-3254. www.mass.gov/dcr. Free admission. Parking $5 (cash only). Daily 8am–sunset.*

Walden Pond.

Salem

1. Salem Witch Museum
2. Peabody Essex Museum
3. Atrium Café
4. Salem Maritime National Historic Site
5. The House of the Seven Gables
6. In a Pig's Eye

If you know Salem only because of its association with witches, you're in for a delightful surprise. Salem has been haunted (sorry) by the witch trials since 1692, but it has far more to offer: It was a center of merchant shipping at the height of the post–Revolutionary War China trade, and today the city celebrates its maritime history at the same time that it preserves and honors the memory of the victims of the witch trials. START: **From downtown Boston, take I-93 north to I-95 north, or take the Callahan Tunnel to Route 1A and follow it to Route 1 north. (The hotel staff can tell you which approach is easier.) From I-95 or Route 1, follow the signs to Route 128 north. Exit at Route 114 east, and follow the signs to downtown Salem. From Boston, the trip takes about 45 minutes if it isn't rush hour.**

① ★★ kids **Salem Witch Museum.** Start here for an excellent overview of the 1692 witch-trial hysteria. The museum centers on a well-researched audiovisual presentation—basically a series of dioramas, populated with life-size human figures, that light up in sequence as recorded narration describes the pertinent events. The story gets a little scary (one of the convicted "witches" was pressed to death by stones piled on a board on his chest), but the anti-prejudice

The Salem Witch Museum building used to be a church.

message is both clear and timeless. 🕐 *1 hr. 19½ Washington Sq. (Rte. 1A and Brown St.).* ☎ *978/744-1692. www.salemwitchmuseum.com. Admission $6.50 adults, $6 seniors, $4.50 kids 6–14, free for kids under 6. Daily July–Aug 10am–7pm; Sept–June 10am–5pm; check ahead for extended Oct hours.*

② ★★ **Peabody Essex Museum.** The Peabody Essex is one of the best art museums in New England, with a growing national reputation that rests in large part on its extensive collections of American art and architecture, maritime art, Asian export art, and Asian, African, and Native American art. In a sizable expansion completed in 2003, the museum gained a wing designed by the internationally renowned architect Moshe Safdie. The addition adjoins perhaps the best-known object in the museum: an 18th-century Qing dynasty house. Yin Yu Tang, as the house is known, was shipped to Salem from rural China. The only example of Chinese domestic architecture outside that country, the house allows an intriguing look at 2 centuries of life in China. Be sure to pick up an audio tour before exploring the house. Also be sure to peek at some of the lower-profile holdings: The museum originated as a maritime museum (the Peabody) and the county historical society (the Essex Institute), and some of my favorite

objects date to those days. I especially like the collections of ship figureheads and the furniture and dollhouses. 🕐 *3 hr. Build your visit around your timed ticket to Yin Yu Tang. East India Sq. (off Hawthorne Blvd. at Essex St.)* ☎ *866/745-1876 or* ☎ *978/745-9500. www.pem.org. Admission $13 adults, $11 seniors, $9 students, free for kids under 17. Yin Yu Tang admission $4 with museum admission. Daily 10am–5pm.*

③ Atrium Café. You don't have to leave the museum to grab a bite—say, a sandwich, salad, or cookie. The airy self-serve cafe, operated by an excellent caterer, makes a good place to stop and strategize. *East India Sq.* ☎ *978/745-9500, ext. 3118. $.*

A bedroom in the Yin Yu Tang at the Peabody Essex Museum.

4 ★ kids **Salem Maritime National Historic Site.** The displays at the National Park Service's waterfront center, in a renovated warehouse, concentrate on the city's seagoing history. Just outside the center is a memorable exhibit: a ship. A 171-foot (52m) (full-size) replica of a 1797 East Indiaman merchant vessel, the *Friendship* is open to visitors on the guided ranger tour; you can also study it from the shore if you don't want to climb on. The tour visits several other buildings and touches on Salem's literary history (Nathaniel Hawthorne once worked in the Custom House), but the high point is that fascinating ship. ⏱ *1 hr. 174 Derby St. (Orange and Kosciusko sts.)* ☎ *978/740-1660. www.nps.gov/sama. Free admission. Guided tours $5 adults, $3 seniors and kids 6–15. Daily 9am–5pm.*

5 ★ kids **The House of the Seven Gables.** Nathaniel Hawthorne wrote the 1851 novel that inspired the name of this attraction, and if you haven't read it since high school (or haven't read it at all), I'm here to tell you: It's *scary.* Don't worry if you can't quite recall the story; begin your visit with the

The House of the Seven Gables belonged to one of Hawthorne's cousins.

audiovisual program that recaps the book (and—fair warning—gives away the ending). The rambling 1668 house holds six rooms of period furniture, including pieces referred to in the novel. Guides point them out on the tour, which includes interesting descriptions of what life in the 1700s was like. The high point of the tour is the secret staircase, but one of my favorite things about visiting this property is the opportunity to poke around the grounds after the tour. The modest home where Hawthorne was born has been moved here, and

The "sky well" of the Yin Yu Tang.

Salem: **Practical Matters**

Driving offers the most flexibility, but Salem is also accessible by public transit and easy to negotiate on foot. The **MBTA** (☎ 800/392-6100 or ☎ 617/222-3200; www.mbta.com) operates commuter trains from North Station and buses from Haymarket; check schedules early in the planning process. Tourist information is widely available; good sources are the **National Park Service Regional Visitor Center,** 2 New Liberty St. (☎ 978/740-1650; www.nps.gov/sama), open daily from 9am to 5pm, and the **Salem Chamber of Commerce,** 63A Wharf St. (☎ 978/744-0004; www.salem-chamber.org), open weekdays from 9am to 5pm. Download or request a visitor's guide from **Destination Salem,** 54 Turner St. (☎ 877/SALEM-MA or ☎ 978/744-3663; www.salem.org).

the lovely period gardens overlook the harbor. ⏱ 1½ hrs. 54 Turner St. (off Derby St.) ☎ 978/744-0991. www.7gables.org. Guided tour of house and grounds $12 adults, $11 seniors, $7.25 kids 5–12, free for kids under 5. Surcharges may apply for special exhibitions. July–Oct daily 10am–7pm; Nov–June daily 10am–5pm. Closed 1st 3 weeks of Jan.

6 ★★ **In a Pig's Eye.** After a busy day of sightseeing, unwind at this friendly neighborhood tavern with a wide-ranging menu (including Mexican specialties Mon–Tues). 148 Derby St. (Daniels St.) ☎ 978/741-4436. $–$$.

Plymouth

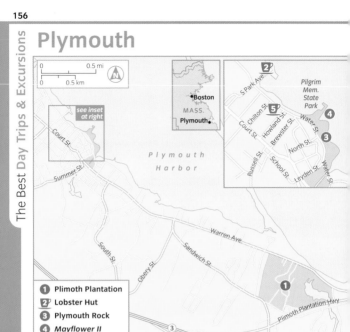

0   0.5 mi
0   0.5 km

Plymouth Harbor

see inset
at right

Court St.

Summer St.

South St.

Obery St.

Sandwich St.

Warren Ave.

Plymouth Plantation Hwy.

Boston
MASS.
Plymouth

Pilgrim
Mem.
State
Park

S. Park Ave.

Chilton St.

Court St.

Howland St.

Brewster St.

Russell St.

School St.

North St.

Leyden St.

Water St.

Water St.

1 Plimoth Plantation
2 Lobster Hut
3 Plymouth Rock
4 *Mayflower II*
5 Peaceful Meadows Ice Cream

Did you wear a construction-paper hat or a feathered head-dress in the Thanksgiving pageant? If you attended grade school in the United States before the heyday of political correctness, you probably did—and you probably know a little something about Plymouth. The Pilgrims. The *Mayflower*. The Rock. Refreshingly, this town honors its history but isn't trapped in the past; it's a lively contemporary community that happens to have a lot of historic attractions. **START: Take I-93 south and merge onto Route 3 south. To go directly to Plimoth Plantation, take Exit 4. Exit 6A deposits you on Route 44 east, which leads straight to downtown Plymouth. If it isn't rush hour, the trip from Boston takes about an hour.**

1 ★★ kids Plimoth Plantation. Until we perfect time travel, a visit here is the best way to experience the Pilgrims' daily life. A re-creation of a 1627 village, Plimoth Plantation approximates the conditions in the early days of the little community, which was settled in 1620. Visitors wander around the farm area, visiting homes and gardens constructed with careful attention to historic detail. The "Pilgrims" are actors who assume the personalities of members of the original community, and they take their roles seriously—kids get a kick out their mystified reactions to questions about innovations such as TV or

Period actors stroll the grounds of Plimoth Plantation.

airplanes. You can watch them framing a house, splitting wood, shearing sheep, preserving foodstuffs, or cooking over an open hearth, all as it was done in the 1600s and using only the tools and cookware available then. Sometimes you can join the activities—perhaps planting, harvesting, witnessing a trial, or visiting a wedding party. You'll be walking a lot, so wear comfortable shoes. If you plan to visit the *Mayflower II* (later in this tour), buy a combination ticket—you'll save a few dollars. 🕑 *3 hr. Be here when the gates open, especially in summer, when morning is the only cool part of the day. 137 Warren Ave. (Rte. 3).* ☎ *508/746-1622. www.plimoth.org. Admission (good for 2 consecutive days) $21 adults, $18 seniors, $12 kids 6–12. Plimoth Plantation and Mayflower II admission $24 adults, $21 seniors and students, $14 kids 6–12, free for kids under 6, $72 families. Apr–Nov daily 9am–5pm. Closed Dec–Mar.*

2 ★ kids **Lobster Hut.** The deck overlooking the harbor is the place to be at this self-service seafood restaurant, which is popular with out-of-towners and locals alike.

25 Town Wharf (off Water St). ☎ *508/746-2270. $–$$.*

3 ★★ kids **Plymouth Rock.** Talk about truth in advertising—this is Plymouth, and that's a rock. But what a rock! Tradition tells us that the original rock was the landing place of the *Mayflower* passengers in 1620. From a hunk 15 feet (5m) long and 3 feet (.9m) wide, it diminished over the years and several relocations. In 1867, the remaining rock wound up here, perched at tide level on the peaceful shore. It's a model attraction: easy to understand, quick to visit, and unexpectedly affecting. In honor of the tercentennial of the Pilgrims' arrival, the Colonial Dames of America commissioned the enclosure, a temple-like structure designed by McKim, Mead & White. 🕑 *10 min. Pilgrim Memorial State Park, Water St. (Leyden and North sts.).* ☎ *508/866-2580. Daily 24 hr.*

Plymouth Rock.

4 ★ kids ***Mayflower II.*** Every time I come here, it hits me again: This ship is *tiny.* A full-scale reproduction of the type of vessel that brought the Pilgrims to America in

Exhibits aboard Mayflower II describe and illustrate the Pilgrims' journey and experience.

1620, *Mayflower II* is just 106½ feet (32m) long. Costumed guides assume the characters of passengers to discuss the vessel and its perilous voyage, while other interpreters provide a contemporary perspective. This is a great place to introduce children to the idea that what they think of as boring history is a true story—about real people. To start, ask them to imagine sharing the tiny *Mayflower* with 101 other people. 🕐 *1 hr. State Pier.* ☎ *508/746-1622. www.plimoth.org. Admission $8 adults, $7 seniors, $6 kids 6–12. Plimoth Plantation (good for 2 consecutive days) and* Mayflower II *admission $24 adults, $21 seniors and students, $14 kids 6–12, free for kids under 6, $72 families. Apr–Nov daily 9am–5pm. Closed Dec–Mar.*

5C ★ **kids** **Peaceful Meadows Ice Cream.** A family business that dates to 1962, Peaceful Meadows is a tasty place to refuel. Take your ice cream (fresh peach—yum!) across the street for a front-row seat along the water. *114 Water St. (Chilton and Howland sts.).* ☎ *508/747-2248. $.* ●

Plymouth: **Practical Matters**

Driving to Plymouth is vastly preferable to taking public transit. Leave plenty of time if you don't drive; the **MBTA** commuter rail (☎ 800/392-6100 or ☎ 617/222-3200; www.mbta.com) from Boston's South Station serves Cordage Park, north of downtown Plymouth, and the local bus (☎ 508/746-0378; www.gatra.org/pal.htm) takes you the rest of the way. There's a year-round visitor information center at Exit 5 off Route 3 that covers the whole region; for Plymouth-specific information, visit the seasonal **visitor center** at 130 Water St. (☎ 508/747-7525), across from the town pier. Information is available year-round from **Destination Plymouth,** 170 Water St. (☎ 800/USA-1620 or ☎ 508/747-7533; www.visit-plymouth.com).

The
Savvy Traveler

Before You Go

Tourist Offices

Contact the **Greater Boston Convention & Visitors Bureau,** 2 Copley Place, Suite 105, Boston, MA 02116-6501 (☎ 888/SEE-BOSTON or ☎ 617/536-4100, ☎ 0171/431-3434 in the U.K.; fax 617/424-7664; www.bostonusa.com), for tons of information online and by mail. Other good resources include the **Cambridge Office for Tourism,** 4 Brattle Street, Suite 208, Cambridge, MA 02138 (☎ 800/862-5678 or ☎ 617/441-2884; fax 617/441-7736; www.cambridge-usa.org), and the **Massachusetts Office of Travel and Tourism,** 10 Park Plaza, Suite 4510, Boston, MA 02116 (☎ 800/447-MASS or ☎ 617/973-8500; fax 617/973-8525; www.massvacation.com).

The Best Times to Go

Conventions, special events, and school vacations make Boston busy virtually year-round. The best weather and largest crowds coincide during foliage season, from mid-September to early November. Spring is unpredictable (snow sometimes falls in April) but overall has smaller crowds than the fall and decent weather. July and August are family vacation time, with large crowds at most attractions. The "slow" season is January through March, when many hotels offer great deals, especially on weekends.

Festivals & Special Events

SPRING. The third Monday of April is **Patriot's Day,** a state holiday that commemorates the events of April 18 and 19, 1775, when the Revolutionary War began. Ceremonies and reenactments take place in Boston's North End at the **Old North Church** (☎ 617/523-6676; www.oldnorth. com) and the **Paul Revere House** (☎ 617/523-2338; www.paulrevere house.org). In suburban Lexington, a skirmish breaks out on the field now known as the Battle Green, and battle rages at the North Bridge in Concord. Contact the **Lexington Chamber of Commerce Visitor Center** (☎ 781/862-1450; www.lexingtonchamber. org) or the **Concord Chamber of Commerce** (☎ 978/369-3120; www. concordmachamber.org) for information. Outside of New England, Patriot's Day is probably best known as the day of the **Boston Marathon** (www.bostonmarathon.org), one of the oldest and most famous in the world. The race begins in Hopkinton, Massachusetts, and ends on Boylston Street just outside Boston's Copley Square. The lead runners break the tape around 2pm. On the Saturday before Patriot's Day, the **Swan Boats** (☎ 617/522-1966; www.swanboats. com) in the Public Garden open their season. The second or third weekend of May brings **Lilac Sunday** to the Arnold Arboretum (☎ 617/524-1717; www.arboretum.harvard.edu). It's the only day of the year that the arboretum allows picnicking.

SUMMER. The second week of June culminates in the **Boston Pride March** (☎ 617/262-9405; www. bostonpride.org), the largest gay pride parade in New England. June is party season in Cambridge, which follows Harvard's gargantuan graduation ceremonies with three entertaining events. Teams participating in the **Dragon Boat Festival** (☎ 617/349-4380; www.boston dragonboat.org), on the Charles River near Harvard Square, compete for a ticket to the national championships; the spectators on the riverbank celebrate Chinese culture and food. The **Central Square World's**

Fair (☎ 617/868-3247; www.
cambridgema.gov) is a large but
standard street festival with an
excellent twist: live performances
by local and national rock, jazz, and
blues musicians. Another arts-oriented event is the **Cambridge River
Festival** (☎ 617/349-4380; www.
cambridgeartscouncil.org), on the
banks of the Charles. The high point
of the summer calendar is **Boston
Harborfest** (☎ 617/227-1528;
www.bostonharborfest.com), the
city's weeklong Fourth of July party.
Events include concerts, children's
activities, cruises, fireworks, the
Boston Chowderfest, guided tours,
talks, and USS *Constitution*'s turn-
around cruise. The big day ends
with a beloved tradition, the **Boston
Pops Concert and Fireworks
Display** (www.july4th.org). The
musicians are on the stage at the
Hatch Shell, on the Esplanade; the
spectators spread out along both
banks of the river and the bridges
across the Charles River basin. The
program includes the *1812 Over-
ture*, with real cannon fire and
church bells. The North End is home
to another tradition, the **Italian-
American feasts** that dominate
weekends in late July and through
August. The street fairs feature live
music, dancing, carnival food, tacky
souvenirs, and lively crowds of

locals and out-of-towners happily
mingling. The two biggest events
are the Fisherman's Feast (www.
fishermansfeast.com) and the Feast
of St. Anthony (www.saintanthonys
feast.com), on consecutive weekends in mid- and late August.

AUTUMN. On the third weekend of
October, the **Head of the Charles
Regatta** (☎ 617/868-6200; www.
hocr.org) dominates Cambridge and,
to a lesser extent, Boston. Rowing
teams and individuals vie to beat the
clock (they start one at a time, not
all together) as they race from the
Charles River basin to West Cambridge. Hundreds of thousands of
fans line the shore and the bridges.
October is party time in Salem,
where **Haunted Happenings**
(☎ 877/SALEM-MA; www.haunted
happenings.org) lasts all month.
Halloween celebrations include
parades, parties, a special commuter-
rail ride from Boston, fortunetelling,
cruises, and tours.

WINTER. Boston's holiday season
begins the day after Thanksgiving,
when Boston Ballet kicks off
its annual performances of *The
Nutcracker* (www.bostonballet.org;
for tickets, ☎ 617/695-6955 or
www.telecharge.com). In mid-
December, the **Boston Tea Party
Reenactment** at the Old South

Useful Websites

- **Boston.com** (the *Boston Globe*): www.boston.com
- **Bostonist:** www.bostonist.com
- **Boston-to-English Dictionary:** www.boston-online.com/
  glossary.html
- **Citysearch:** http://boston.citysearch.com
- **MBTA** (subway, trolley, bus, ferry, and commuter-rail schedules
  and route maps): www.mbta.com
- **National Park Service:** www.nps.gov
- **Open Table** (restaurant reservations): www.opentable.com

BOSTON'S AVERAGE TEMPERATURES & RAINFALL						
	JAN	FEB	MAR	APR	MAY	JUNE
Temp. (°F)	30	31	38	49	59	68
Temp. (°C)	-1	-1	3	9	15	20
Rainfall (in.)	4.0	3.7	4.1	3.7	3.5	2.9
	JULY	AUG	SEPT	OCT	NOV	DEC
Temp. (°F)	74	72	65	55	45	34
Temp. (°C)	23	22	18	13	7	1
Rainfall (in.)	2.7	3.7	3.4	3.4	4.2	4.9

Meeting House (☎ 617/482-6439; www.oldsouthmeetinghouse.org) enlists audience members in the debate over taxation without representation and brings history alive. When it's open (it was closed for renovation at press time, with plans to reopen in 2007), the Boston Tea Party Ship and Museum on the Congress Street Bridge (☎ 617/338-1773; www.bostonteapartyship. com) is the second stop on the reenactment circuit. The **Black Nativity,** poet Langston Hughes's "gospel opera," employs a cast of more than 100 on most December weekends. Shows are at Converse Hall, Tremont Temple Baptist Church, 88 Tremont Street (☎ 617/723-3486; www.blacknativity.org). Another traditional show, the **Christmas Revels** (☎ 617/972-8300; www.revels.org), takes place at Harvard's Sanders Theatre (☎ 617/496-2222). A multicultural celebration of the winter solstice, it celebrates the customs of a different culture each year. The year ends with a bang: **First Night** (☎ 617/542-1399; www.firstnight.org) and its double fireworks. Boston's party is the original arts-oriented, no-alcohol, citywide New Year's Eve celebration. It begins in the early afternoon and includes a parade, ice sculptures, art exhibitions, theatrical performances, and indoor and outdoor entertainment. Fireworks

bloom over Boston Common at 7pm and over Boston Harbor at midnight.

The Weather

New England weather is famously changeable-variations from day to day and even hour to hour can be enormous. Always dress in layers. Spring and fall are the best bets for moderate temperatures, but spring (also known as mud season) doesn't usually settle in until early May. Summers are hot, especially in July and August, and can be uncomfortably humid. Fall is when you're most likely to catch a comfortable run of dry, sunny days and cool nights. Winters are cold and usually snowy-bring a warm coat and sturdy boots.

Cellphones

Cellphones (mobiles) with tri-band GSM capabilities work in the United States; call your service provider before departing your home country to ensure that the international call bar has been switched off and to check call charges, which can be extremely high. Also remember that you will be charged for calls you receive on a U.K. mobile used abroad. U.K. visitors can rent a U.S. phone before leaving home. Contact **Cellhire** (☎ 0800/610-610; www. cellhire.co.uk). One good wireless-rental company is **InTouch USA** (☎ 800/872-7626 or ☎ 703/222-7161; www.intouchglobal.com).

Car Rentals

For booking rental cars online, the best deals are usually on rental-car company websites. U.K. visitors should check **Holidayautos** (online only; www.holidayautos.co.uk). Companies with offices at Boston's Logan Airport include **Alamo** (☎ 800/327-9633; www.goalamo.com), **Avis** (☎ 800/831-2847; www.avis.com), **Budget** (☎ 800/527-0700; www.budget.com), **Dollar** (☎ 800/800-4000; www.dollar.com), **Hertz** (☎ 800/654-3131; www.hertz.com), and **National** (☎ 800/227-7368; www.nationalcar.com). **Enterprise** (☎ 800/325-8007; www.enterprise.com) and **Thrifty** (☎ 800/367-2277; www.thrifty.com) are nearby but not on the grounds.

Getting **There**

By Plane

Boston's Logan International Airport (usually called "Logan"; airport code BOS) is in East Boston at the end of the Sumner, Callahan, and Ted Williams tunnels, 3 miles (4.8km) across the harbor from downtown. For a preview and real-time flight arrival and departure information, visit the website (www.massport.com/logan). Wireless Internet access is available all over the airport for $8 a day through Logan WiFi (☎ 617/561-9434; www.loganwifi.com).

Getting to & from the Airport
General Info: The Massachusetts Port Authority, or MassPort (☎ 800/23-LOGAN; www.massport.com), coordinates airport transportation. The toll-free line provides information about getting to the city and to many nearby suburbs. It's available 24 hours a day and is staffed weekdays from 8am to 7pm.

Taxis: Just getting into a cab at the airport costs $8.25 ($6.50 in fees plus the initial $1.75 fare). The total fare to downtown or the Back Bay runs $20 to $30. Depending on traffic, the driver might use the Ted Williams Tunnel for destinations outside downtown, such as the Back Bay.

Public Transit: The Silver Line bus stops at each airport terminal and runs directly to South Station, where you can connect to the Red Line subway and the commuter rail to the southern suburbs. It takes about 20 minutes, not including waiting time. The subway takes just 10 minutes to reach downtown; free shuttle buses run from each terminal to the Airport station on the Blue Line of the T from 5:30am to 1am every day, year-round. The Blue Line stops at Aquarium, State Street, and Government Center, downtown points where you can exit or transfer to the other lines. The bus or subway fare was $1.25 at press time.

Ferries & Boats: The trip to the downtown waterfront in a weather-protected **boat** takes about 7 minutes and costs $10 one-way. The free no. 66 shuttle bus connects the airport terminals to the Logan ferry dock. **Harbor Express** (☎ 617/222-6999; www.harborexpress.com), runs to Long Wharf, behind the Marriott Long Wharf hotel. The **City Water Taxi** (☎ 617/422-0392; www.citywatertaxi.com) connects about a dozen stops on the harbor, including the airport ferry dock. The **Rowes Wharf Water Taxi** (☎ 617/406-8584; www.roweswharfwatertaxi.com) serves Rowes Wharf, off Atlantic Avenue behind the Boston Harbor Hotel. Call ahead from the dock for water-taxi pickup.

Shuttle Vans: The Logan Airport website (www.massport.com/logan) lists numerous companies that serve local hotels. One-way prices start at $12 per person and are subject to fuel surcharges as gas prices fluctuate.

By Car

Three major highways converge in Boston. **I-90,** also known as the Massachusetts Turnpike ("Mass. Pike," to the locals), is an east-west toll road that originates at Logan Airport and links up with the New York State Thruway. **I-93/U.S. 1** extends north to Canada. **I-93/Route 3,** the Southeast Expressway, connects Boston with the south, including Cape Cod. To avoid driving downtown, exit the Mass. Pike at Cambridge/Allston or at the Prudential Center in the Back Bay. **I-95** (Massachusetts Rte. 128) is a beltway about 11 miles (17.7km) from downtown that connects Boston to highways in Rhode Island, Connecticut, and New York to the south, and New Hampshire and Maine to the north.

The approach to Cambridge is **Storrow Drive** or **Memorial Drive,** which run along either side of the Charles River. Storrow Drive has a Harvard Square exit that leads across the Anderson Bridge to John F. Kennedy Street and into the square. Memorial Drive intersects with Kennedy Street; turn away from the bridge to reach the square.

By Train & Bus

Boston has three rail centers: **South Station,** on Atlantic Avenue at Summer Street; **Back Bay Station,** on Dartmouth Street between Huntington and Columbus avenues; and **North Station,** on Causeway Street. **Amtrak** (☎ 800/USA-RAIL or ☎ 617/482-3660; www.amtrak.com) serves all train stations, which are also linked to the MBTA subway.

The bus terminal, formally the **South Station Transportation Center,** is on Atlantic Avenue next to the train station. The largest of the bus lines that serve Boston are **Greyhound** (☎ 800/231-2222 or ☎ 617/526-1800; www.greyhound.com) and **Peter Pan** (☎ 800/343-9999; www.peterpanbus.com).

Getting **Around**

On Foot

This is the way to go if you can manage it. Even the tallest hills aren't too steep, and vehicular traffic is brutal.

By Public Transportation

The **Massachusetts Bay Transportation Authority,** or MBTA (☎ 800/392-6100 or ☎ 617/222-3200; www.mbta.com) runs subways, trolleys, buses, and ferries in Boston and many suburbs, as well as the commuter rail, which extends as far as Providence, Rhode Island. The system is phasing in automated fare collection to replace tokens, which are worth $1.25 and should be obsolete by mid-2007. At press time, fares were set to increase in 2007, but they weren't set. Expect to pay at least $1.50 for the subway and $1 for the bus.

The subways (called "the T" by locals) are color-coded: the Red, Green, Blue, and Orange lines. The commuter rail to the suburbs is purple on system maps and sometimes called the Purple Line. The Silver Line is a fancy name for a bus line. Service begins at around 5:15am and ends around 12:30am.

Buses and "trackless trolleys" (buses with electric antennae) provide service around town and to and around the suburbs. The Silver Line looks like a branch of the subway on some maps and on the MBTA website but is a bus line.

The Boston Harbor water shuttle (☎ 617/227-4321) is a commuter ferry that connects Long Wharf, near the New England Aquarium, with the Charlestown Navy Yard. The one-way fare is $1.50.

City Water Taxi (☎ 617/422-0392; www.citywatertaxi.com) offers on-call service in small boats that connect a dozen stops on the Inner Harbor, including the airport. One-way fares start at $10. The **Rowes Wharf Water Taxi** (☎ 617/406-8584) connects the airport ferry dock, the federal courthouse in Fan Pier, the World Trade Center, and Rowes Wharf, off Atlantic Avenue behind the Boston Harbor Hotel. The flat fare is $10 one-way. Call ahead from the dock for pickup by either service. **Seaport Express** (☎ 617/939-4802; www.seaporttma.org), connects Central Wharf, behind the New England Aquarium, to the Seaport World Trade Center on the South Boston waterfront. The one-way fare is $1.50.

By Taxi

Taxis can be tough to hail on the street; your best bet is to call a dispatcher or seek out a hotel or cabstand. To call ahead, try the **Independent Taxi Operators Association,** or ITOA (☎ 617/426-8700); **Boston Cab** (☎ 617/536-5010 or ☎ 617/262-2227); **Town Taxi** (☎ 617/536-5000); or **Metro Cab** (☎ 617/242-8000). In Cambridge, call **Ambassador Brattle** (☎ 617/492-1100) or **Yellow Cab** (☎ 617/547-3000).

By Car

If you plan to visit only Boston and Cambridge, there's absolutely no reason to have a car. With its pricey parking and narrow, one-way streets, not to mention abundant construction, Boston in particular is a motorist's nightmare. Drive to Cambridge only if you're feeling flush-you'll pay to park there, too. If you arrive by car, park at the hotel and use the car for day trips. If you want to rent a car for day trips, see "Car Rentals," earlier in this chapter, for more information.

Fast **Facts**

Area Codes   Eastern Massachusetts has eight area codes: Boston proper, **617** and **857**; immediate suburbs, **781** and **339**; northern and western suburbs, **978** and **351**; southern suburbs, **508** and **774**. To make a local call, you must dial all 10 digits.

ATMs/Cashpoints   Before you leave home, find out your daily withdrawal limit. Unless you can find an ATM operated by your own bank, expect to pay a $1 to $3 access fee.

Cirrus (☎ 800/424-7787; www.mastercard.com), **PLUS** (☎ 800/843-7587; www.visa.com), and **NYCE** (☎ 888/456-2844; www.nyce.net) cover most Boston-area banks.

Babysitters   Many hotels maintain lists of babysitters; check at the front desk or with the concierge. Local agencies aren't a cost-effective option; most charge a steep annual fee on top of the daily referral charge and the sitter's hourly wage and expenses. If you're in town on business, ask whether the company you're visiting has a corporate membership in an agency.

B&Bs Try **Bed & Breakfast Agency of Boston** (☎ 800/248-9262, ☎ 617/720-3540, or ☎ 0800/89-5128 from the U.K.; www.boston-bnbagency.com)

Banking Hours **Most are open weekdays 9am–5pm, and sometimes Saturday morning.**

Climate See "The Weather," earlier in this chapter.

Consulates & Embassies
Embassies are in Washington, D.C. Some consulates are in major U.S. cities, and most nations have a mission to the United Nations in New York City. For addresses and phone numbers of embassies in Washington, D.C., call (☎ 202/555-1212) or visit **www.embassy.org/embassies**. The following are Boston-area addresses for a selection of countries: The **Canadian consulate** is at 3 Copley Place, Suite 400, Boston, MA 02116 (☎ 617/262-3760). The **Irish consulate** is at 535 Boylston St., Boston, MA 02116 (☎ 617/267-9330). The **Japanese consulate** is at Federal Reserve Plaza, 600 Atlantic Ave., 14th Floor, Boston, MA 02210 (☎ 617/973-9772). The **U.K. consulate** is at 1 Memorial Dr., Suite 1500, Cambridge, MA 02142 (☎ 617/245-4500).

Customs International visitors arriving by air, no matter what the port of entry, should cultivate patience and resignation before setting foot on U.S. soil. Clearing immigration control can take as long as 2 hours. People traveling by air from Canada, Bermuda, and certain Caribbean countries can sometimes clear Customs and Immigration at the point of departure, which is much faster.

Dentists The desk staff or concierge at your hotel might be able to suggest a dentist. The **Massachusetts Dental Society**

(☎ 800/342-8747 or ☎ 508/480-9797; www.massdental.org) can point you toward a member.

Doctors The desk staff or concierge at your hotel should be able to direct you to a doctor. You can also try the physician referral service at one of the area's many hospitals. Among them are Brigham and Women's (☎ 800/294-9999) and Massachusetts General (☎ 800/711-4MGH).

Drinking Laws See "Liquor Laws," below.

Electricity Like Canada, the United States uses 110 to 120 volts AC (60 cycles), compared with 220 to 240 volts AC (50 cycles) in most of Europe, Australia, and New Zealand. If your small appliances use 220 to 240 volts, you'll need a 110-volt transformer and a plug adapter with two flat parallel pins to operate them here. Downward converters that change 220-240 volts to 110-120 volts are difficult to find in the United States, so bring one with you.

Embassies See "Consulates & Embassies," above.

Emergencies Call ☎ 911 for fire, ambulance, or the Boston, Brookline, or Cambridge police. This is a free call from pay phones. For the state police, call ☎ 617/523-1212, or ☎ *77 from a cellphone. The toll-free number for the **Poison Control Center** is ☎ 800/682-9211. If you encounter serious problems, call or visit **Travelers Aid Family Services,** 17 East St., Boston, MA 02111 (☎ 617/542-7286; www.taboston.org), across Atlantic Avenue from South Station.

Holidays Banks, government offices, post offices, and some stores, restaurants, and museums close on the following legal national holidays: January 1 (New Year's Day), the third Monday in January (Martin Luther King Day), the third Monday in February (Presidents' Day, Washington's Birthday), the last

Monday in May (Memorial Day), July 4th (Independence Day), the first Monday in September (Labor Day), the second Monday in October (Columbus Day), November 11 (Veterans Day/Armistice Day), the fourth Thursday in November (Thanksgiving Day), and December 25 (Christmas Day). Also, the Tuesday following the first Monday in November is Election Day and is a federal government holiday in presidential-election years (held every four years, next in 2008). In Massachusetts, state offices close for Patriot's Day on the third Monday in April, and Suffolk County offices (including Boston City Hall) close on March 17 for Evacuation Day.

Insurance   For Domestic Visitors: Trip-cancellation insurance helps you get your money back if you have to back out of a trip or depart early, or if your travel supplier goes bankrupt. Permissible reasons for trip cancellation can range from sickness to natural disasters to the State Department's declaring a destination unsafe for travel. Make sure your airline or cruise line is on the list of carriers covered in case of bankruptcy. For more information, contact one of the following insurers: **Access America** (☎ 866/807-3982; www.access america.com); **Travel Guard International** (☎ 800/826-4919; www. travelguard.com); **Travel Insured International** (☎ 800/243-3174; www.travelinsured.com); or **Travelex Insurance Services** (☎ 888/457-4602; www.travelex-insurance.com).

Medical Insurance: Good policies will cover the costs of an accident, repatriation, or death. Packages such as **Europ Assistance's "Worldwide Healthcare Plan"** are sold by European automobile clubs and travel agencies at attractive rates. **Worldwide Assistance Services, Inc.** (☎ 800/777-8710; www.worldwide assistance.com) is the agent for Europ Assistance in the United

States. Although it's not required of travelers, health insurance is highly recommended. International visitors should note that unlike many European countries, the United States does not usually offer free or low-cost medical care to its citizens or visitors. Doctors and hospitals are expensive, and in most cases will require advance payment or proof of insurance coverage before they will render their services. Though lack of insurance may prevent you from being admitted to a hospital in nonemergencies, don't worry about being left on a street corner to die: The American way is to fix you now and bill the living daylights out of you later.

Insurance   For British Travelers: Most big travel agents offer their own insurance and will probably try to sell you their package when you book a holiday. Think before you sign. **Britain's Consumers' Association** recommends that you insist on seeing the policy and reading the fine print before buying travel insurance. **The Association of British Insurers** (☎ 020/7600-3333; www. abi.org.uk) gives advice by phone and publishes *Holiday Insurance,* a free guide to policy provisions and prices. You might also shop around for better deals: Try **Columbus Direct** (☎ 0870/033-9988; www. columbusdirect.net). **Insurance for Canadian Travelers:** Check with your provincial health plan offices or call **Health Canada** (☎ 866/225-0709; www.hc-sc.gc.ca) to find out the extent of your coverage and what documentation and receipts you must take home in case you are treated in the United States. **Insurance for Australian Travelers: Online Travel Insurance** (☎ 07/3283-7533; www.travelinsurance australia.com.au) offers a variety of policies for U.S. travel.

Lost-Luggage Insurance: On flights within the United States, checked baggage is covered up to

$2,500 per ticketed passenger. On international flights (and U.S. portions of international trips), baggage coverage is limited to approximately $9 per pound, up to approximately $635 per checked bag. If you plan to check items more valuable than what's covered by the standard liability, see if your homeowner's policy covers your valuables, get baggage insurance as part of your comprehensive travel-insurance package, or buy Travel Guard's "Bag-Trak" product. Take valuables and irreplaceable items with you in your carry-on luggage; airline policies don't cover many valuables, including money and electronics. If your luggage is lost, immediately file a lost-luggage claim at the airport, detailing the luggage contents. Most airlines require that you report delayed, damaged, or lost baggage within 4 hours of arrival. The airlines are required to deliver luggage, once found, directly to your house or destination free of charge.

Hospitals   **Massachusetts General Hospital,** 55 Fruit St. (☎ 617/726-2000), and **Tufts-New England Medical Center,** 750 Washington St. (☎ 617/636-5000), are closest to downtown. At the Harvard Medical Area on the Boston-Brookline border are **Beth Israel Deaconess Medical Center,** 330 Brookline Ave. (☎ 617/667-7000); **Brigham and Women's Hospital,** 75 Francis St. (☎ 617/732-5500); and **Children's Hospital,** 300 Longwood Ave. (☎ 617/355-6000). In Cambridge are **Mount Auburn Hospital,** 330 Mount Auburn St. (☎ 617/492-3500), and **Cambridge Hospital,** 1493 Cambridge St. (☎ 617/498-1000).

Internet   Boston has few cybercafes, but many coffee shops and other businesses offer wireless access (free or for a fee). Your hotel might have a terminal for guest use, and many hotels offer on-premises

wireless access (often for a daily fee). The ubiquitous **FedEx Kinko's** charges 10¢ to 20¢ a minute. Locations include 2 Center Plaza, Government Center (☎ 617/973-9000); 10 Post Office Sq., Financial District (☎ 617/482-4400); 187 Dartmouth St., Back Bay (☎ 617/262-6188); and 1 Mifflin Place, off Mount Auburn Street near Eliot Street, Harvard Square (☎ 617/497-0125). **Tech Superpowers,** 252 Newbury St., 3rd floor (☎ 617/267-9716; www.newburyopen.net), also offers access by the hour ($5/hr.; $3 minimum).

Limos   Try **Carey Limousine Boston** (☎ 800/336-4646 or ☎ 617/623-8700), **Commonwealth Limousine Service** (☎ 800/558-LIMO or ☎ 617/787-1110), or **Dav-El of Boston** (☎ 800/343-2071 or ☎ 617/884-2600).

Liquor Laws   The legal drinking age in Massachusetts (and the rest of the U.S.) is 21. Many bars, particularly those near college campuses, check the ID of everyone who enters. Liquor stores and the liquor sections of other stores are open Monday through Saturday and open at noon on Sunday in communities where that's legal. Last call typically is 30 minutes before closing time (1am in bars, 2am in clubs).

Mail & Postage   Domestic postage rates are 24¢ for a postcard and 39¢ for a letter. For international mail, a first-class letter of up to ½ ounce costs 84¢ (63¢ to Canada and Mexico), a first-class postcard costs 75¢ (55¢ to Canada and Mexico), and a preprinted postal aerogramme costs 75¢. The main post office, at 25 Dorchester Ave. (☎ 617/654-5302), next to South Station, is open daily 24 hours.

Money   **Traveler's checks:** You can buy traveler's checks at most banks. **American Express** offers them in denominations of $20, $50, $100, $500, and (for cardholders) $1,000. You'll pay a service charge ranging from 1% to 4%. Buy Amex checks over the phone by calling ☎ 800/221-7282; ☎ 0870/600-1060 in the U.K.; visit www.american express.com.au in Australia; gold and platinum cardholders who use these numbers are exempt from the 1% fee. AAA members can obtain **Visa** checks for a $9.95 fee (for checks up to $1,500) at most AAA offices or by calling ☎ 866/339-3378. **MasterCard** (☎ 800/223-9920) also offers traveler's checks. If you carry traveler's checks, keep a record of their serial numbers separate from your checks in the event that they are stolen or lost. You'll get a refund faster if you know the numbers.

Parking   Most spaces on the street are metered (and patrolled until at least 6pm Mon-Sat) and are open to nonresidents for 2 hours or less between 8am and 6pm. The penalty is a $40 ticket-even the most expensive garage is cheaper. The rate is usually $1 per hour; bring plenty of quarters. Time limits range from 15 minutes to 2 hours.

A full day at most garages costs no more than $25, but some downtown facilities charge as much as $35, and hourly rates can be exorbitant. Try the city-run garage under **Boston Common** (☎ 617/954-2096); the entrance is on Charles Street between Boylston and Beacon streets. You get a slight break on the price if you buy something at the shopping centers associated with the **Prudential Center** garage (☎ 617/267-1002), with entrances on Boylston Street, Huntington Avenue, and Exeter Street, and at the Sheraton Boston Hotel; the **Copley Place** garage (☎ 617/375-4488), off Huntington Avenue; and the **75 State Street Garage** (☎ 617/742-7275), near Faneuil Hall Marketplace. Good-size garages downtown are at **Government Center** off Congress Street (☎ 617/227-0385), **Sudbury Street** off Congress

Street (☎ 617/973-6954), the **New England Aquarium** (☎ 617/723-1731), and **Zero Post Office Square** in the Financial District (☎ 617/423-1430). In the Back Bay, there's a large facility near the Hynes Convention Center on **Dalton Street** (☎ 617/247-8006).

Passports   Always keep a photocopy of your passport with you when you're traveling. If your passport is lost or stolen, having a copy facilitates the reissuing process at a local consulate or embassy. Keep your passport and other valuables in the hotel or room safe. See "Consulates & Embassies," above, for more information.

Restrooms   The visitor center at 15 State Street has a public restroom, as do most tourist attractions, hotels, department stores, malls, and public buildings. The CambridgeSide Galleria, Copley Place, Prudential Center, and Quincy Market shopping areas and most branches of fast-food restaurants and coffee bars have clean restrooms. Some restaurants and bars, including those in tourist areas, display a sign saying that toilets are for the use of patrons only. Paying for a cup of coffee or a soft drink qualifies you as a patron. You'll find free-standing, self-cleaning **pay toilets** (25¢) at various locations around downtown. Check these facilities carefully before using them; despite regular patrols, IV-drug users have been known to take advantage of the generous time limits.

Safety   Boston and Cambridge are generally safe, but you should always take the same precautions you would in any other large North American city. As in any city, stay out of parks (including Boston Common, the Public Garden, and the Esplanade) at night unless you're in a crowd. Specific areas to avoid at night include Boylston Street between Tremont and Washington streets, and Tremont Street from

Stuart to Boylston streets. Try not to walk alone late at night in the Theater District or on the side streets around North Station. Public transportation in the areas you're likely to visit is busy and safe, but service stops between 12:30am and 1am.

Smoking   Massachusetts is an antitobacco stronghold. State law bans smoking in all workplaces, including restaurants, bars, and clubs.

Taxes   The 5% state sales tax in Massachusetts applies to everything except groceries, prescription drugs, newspapers, and clothing that costs less than $175. The tax on meals and take-out food is 5%. The lodging tax is 12.45% in Boston and Cambridge.

Telephones   For directory assistance or information, dial ☎ 411. Pay phones, which are becoming increasingly scarce, usually charge 35¢ for a 3-minute call.

Tipping   In hotels, tip **bellhops** at least $1 per bag and tip the **chamber staff** at least $2 per day. Tip the **doorman** or **concierge** only for a specific service (for example, calling a cab for you or obtaining difficult-to-get theater tickets). Tip the **valet-parking attendant** $1 every time you get your car. In restaurants, bars, and nightclubs, tip **service staff** 15% to 20% of the check, tip **bartenders** 10% to 15%, and tip **checkroom attendants** $1 per garment. Tip **cab drivers** 15% of the fare, tip **skycaps** at airports at least $1 per bag, and tip **hairdressers** and **barbers** 15% to 20%.

Toilets   See "Restrooms," above.

Tourist Information Offices   The **Boston National Historical Park Visitor Center,** 15 State St. (☎ 617/242-5642; www.nps.gov/bost; daily 9am-5pm), is across the street from the Old State House.

The **Greater Boston Convention & Visitors Bureau** (☎ 888/SEE-BOSTON or ☎ 617/536-4100; www.bostonusa.com) operates the **Boston Common Information Center,** 147 Tremont St., on the Common (Mon-Sat 8:30am-5pm, Sun 9am-5pm) and the **Prudential Information Center,** on the main level of the Prudential Center, 800 Boylston St. (Mon-Fri 8:30am-6pm, Sat-Sun 10am-6pm).

Transit Info   Call ☎ 617/222-3200 for the MBTA (subways, local buses, commuter rail) and ☎ 800/23-LOGAN for the Massachusetts Port Authority (airport transportation).

Travelers with Disabilities   Boston Cab (☎ 617/536-5010) has wheelchair-accessible vehicles; advance notice is recommended. An **Airport Accessible Van** (☎ 617/561-1769) operates within Logan Airport. Newer subway stations are wheelchair accessible; contact the **MBTA** (☎ 800/392-6100 or ☎ 617/222-3200; www.mbta.com) to see if the stations you need are accessible. All MBTA buses have lifts or kneelers; call ☎ 800/LIFT-BUS for more information. To learn more, contact the **Office for Transportation Access,** 145 Dartmouth St., Boston, MA 02116 (☎ 617/222-5438 or ☎ TTY 617/222-5854). An excellent resource is **VSA Arts Massachusetts,** 2 Boylston St., Boston, MA 02116 (☎ 617/350-7713 or ☎ TTY 617/350-6836; www.vsamass.org). It maintains a comprehensive website (www.accessexpressed.net) that provides general access information and specifics about more than 200 cultural facilities across the United States.

Weather   Call ☎ 617/936-1234.

Boston: **A Brief History**

1630 John Winthrop leads settlers to present-day Charlestown. Seeking better water, they push on to Shawmut, which they call Tri-mountain. On September 7, they name it Boston in honor of the English hometown of many Puritans. On October 19, 108 voters attend the first town meeting.

1635 Boston Latin School, America's first public school, opens.

1636 Harvard College is founded.

1638 America's first printing press is established in Cambridge.

1639 The country's first post office opens in Richard Fairbank's home.

1704 America's first regularly published newspaper, the *Boston News Letter,* is founded.

1770 On March 5, five colonists are killed outside what is now the Old State House, an incident soon known as the Boston Massacre.

1773 On December 16, during the Boston Tea Party, colonists dump 342 chests of tea into the harbor from three British ships.

1775 On April 18, Paul Revere and William Dawes spread the word that the British are marching toward Lexington and Concord. The next day, "the shot heard round the world" is fired. On June 17, the British win the Battle of Bunker Hill but suffer heavy casualties.

1776 On March 17, royal troops evacuate by ship. On July 18, the Declaration of Independence is read from the balcony of the Old State House.

1831 William Lloyd Garrison publishes the first issue of the *Liberator,* a newspaper dedicated to emancipation.

1870 The Museum of Fine Arts is founded.

1872 The Great Fire burns 65 acres (65ha), consumes 800 buildings, and kills 33 people.

1876 Boston University professor Alexander Graham Bell invents the telephone.

1881 The Boston Symphony Orchestra is founded.

1895 Boston Public Library opens on Copley Square.

1897 The first Boston Marathon is run. The first subway in America opens-a 1¾-mile (2.8km) stretch beneath Boylston Street.

1918 The Red Sox celebrate their World Series victory; a championship drought begins.

1930s The Great Depression devastates what remains of New England's industrial base.

1946 Boston's First Congressional District sends John F. Kennedy to Congress.

1957 The Boston Celtics win the first of their 16 NBA championships.

1958 The Freedom Trail is mapped out and painted.

1959 Construction of the Prudential Center begins and with it, the transformation of the skyline.

1966 Massachusetts attorney general Edward Brooke, a Republican, becomes the first black elected to the U.S. Senate in the 20th century.

1969 Students protesting the Vietnam War occupy University Hall at Harvard.

1974 Twenty years after the U.S. Supreme Court made school segregation illegal, school busing begins citywide, sparking unrest in Roxbury and Charlestown.

1976 The restored Faneuil Hall Marketplace opens.

1988 The Central Artery/Third Harbor Tunnel Project, better known as the Big Dig, is approved.

1990s The murder rate plummets, the economy booms, and Boston again becomes a "hot" city.

1995 The first complete piece of the Big Dig, the Ted Williams Tunnel, opens.

1999 Busing quietly ends, not with a riot but with a court order.

2000 Engineers announce that Big Dig construction is half complete.

2001 The 2000 Census shows Boston with a population of 589,141-49.5% of which is white. On September 11, both planes used in the terrorist attacks on New York's World Trade Center originate in Boston.

2002 The New England Patriots win the Super Bowl, breaking a drought that dated to 1986 (the Celtics' most recent NBA championship).

2003 The state supreme court rules that forbidding same-sex civil marriage violates the state constitution. The Leonard P. Zakim Bunker Hill Bridge, the signature of the Big Dig and 21st-century Boston, opens to traffic. Demolition of the elevated Central Artery begins.

2004 The Red Sox win the World Series for the first time in 86 years. The Patriots win another Super Bowl. Massachusetts bans workplace smoking. Same-sex marriage becomes law.

2005 The Patriots win yet another Super Bowl. The Red Sox quell rumors by formally announcing that the team will stay at Fenway Park. Boston-based Gillette is acquired by Cincinnati-based Procter & Gamble.

2006 The final piece of the elevated Expressway comes down. The Macy's brand replaces Filene's, the long-time New England department store chain (the Filene's Basement discount chain, a separate company, survives).

Boston **Art & Architecture**

New York has the Statue of Liberty. Paris has the Eiffel Tower. Seattle has the Space Needle. Boston has . . . redbrick.

You'll see many other building materials, of course, but in forming a mental picture of the city, most people return inexorably to redbrick. It's everywhere, from the **Old North Church** (1723) to the **Boston Harbor Hotel** (1987). Those buildings bookend the central waterfront,

irresistibly drawing the eye to their dramatic architecture. The church is small compared with the office towers and condo complexes nearby, but as ever, it dwarfs its closest neighbors. The hotel's landmark archway allows a peek of downtown and, often, of a flag or banner flapping in the courtyard under the huge dome.

Boston's wide variety of architecture makes it a visual treat even as its lack of coherence torments architects. Fashions change, buildings disappear, urban renewal leads to questionable decisions, but everywhere you go, there's something interesting to look at.

Built around 1680, the **Paul Revere House** in the North End is a reminder that for Boston's first 2 centuries, buildings were mostly made of wood, and huge portions of the town regularly burned to the ground. The house is colonial in age but Tudor, rather than typically "colonial," in style. The casement windows and overhanging second floor are medieval features, and when the Reveres moved in, in 1770, the house was no longer fashionable. The one next door would have been: the **Pierce/Hichborn House,** constructed of brick around 1711, is a good example of the Georgian architecture often seen in 18th-century Boston.

After the Revolution, from 1780 to 1820, the Federal style dominated. In Boston the new style was closely associated with architect Charles Bulfinch. His work is all over Boston, most conspicuously in the **State House** (1797) and in many Beacon Hill residences. The new Americans rejected British influence after the war and turned to classical antiquity (filtered through the Scottish architect Robert Adam) for the austere features that characterize the style: Ionic and Corinthian detailing, frequently in white against red brick or clapboard; fanlights over doors; and an almost maniacal insistence on symmetry. In the first **Harrison Gray Otis house** (1796), now the Otis House Museum, at 141 Cambridge St., Bulfinch even devised a room with one false door to balance the real one. Bulfinch also designed

St. Stephen's Church (1804) in the North End, Harvard's **University Hall** (1814), and the central part of Massachusetts General Hospital, now known as **Bulfinch Pavilion** (1818). He also planned the 1805 enlargement of **Faneuil Hall,** which made it three times the size it was when it opened in 1742.

No other architect is as closely associated with Boston as Bulfinch, but in a brief visit you're likely to see just as much of the work of several others. Alexander Parris designed **Quincy Market** (1826), the Greek Revival centerpiece of Faneuil Hall Marketplace. It was renovated and reopened in 1976 for the nation's Bicentennial celebration. Across town, **Trinity Church** (1877), the Romanesque showpiece in Copley Square, is H. H. Richardson's masterwork.

Fascinating architectural areas lie north and south of Copley Square. To the north is the **Back Bay,** built on landfill, which permitted a logical street pattern. The grid-an anomaly in Boston-was planned in the 1860s and 1870s mostly by Arthur Gilman, and the Parisian flavor of the boulevards reflects his interest in French Second Empire style. It's also evident in Gilman's design (with Gridley J. F. Bryant) of **Old City Hall** (1862) on School Street. Its mansard roof is an early example of a style duplicated on hundreds of town houses in the Back Bay. Heading south from Copley Square, you come to the **South End,** another trove of Victoriana whose park-studded layout owes more to London than to Paris.

The architecture of the building boom that started in the 1960s owes a great deal to the fertile mind of a former Harvard instructor, **I. M. Pei.** His firm was responsible for much of the new construction, usually to good effect. The **Christian Science Center** (1973), the **John F. Kennedy Presidential Library and Museum**

(1979), and the **West Wing** of the Museum of Fine Arts (1981) are rousing successes. The **John Hancock Tower** (1974) is the most dramatic point in the Boston skyline, but it began its life by shedding panes of glass onto the street below (the problem has been corrected).

Government Center dates to the early 1960s and is resented by many Bostonians less for its inelegant plainness than because it replaced Scollay Square. That gritty, congested area was filled with theaters, shops, and burlesque houses, and its decrepitude and appeal are recalled with equal affection. Government Center's greatest offense is that it surrounds **City Hall,** a utilitarian monstrosity whose numerous sins are just starting to be corrected.

The vast brick wasteland of City Hall Plaza has been broken up by a small park, but it's still no prize. It does allow you to do a little trick, though: facing the building from the plaza or from Faneuil Hall, hold up the "tails" side of a nickel, upside-down. The resemblance to Monticello (Thomas Jefferson's Virginia estate) is eerie.

The **Big Dig** highway-construction project that dominated the downtown area in the late 20th century and well into the 21st is finally finished. It left behind the Leonard P. Zakim-Bunker Hill Memorial Bridge, the gorgeous white structure that spans the Charles River. The bridge is gaining recognition as a symbol of Boston, but it hasn't quite managed to eclipse our old friend red brick. Maybe it never will.

Toll-Free Numbers and Websites

Airlines
AER LINGUS
☎ 800/474-7424
☎ 3531/886-8844 in Ireland
www.aerlingus.ie
AIR CANADA
☎ 888/247-2262
www.aircanada.com
AIRTRAN AIRLINES
☎ 800/247-8726
www.airtran.com
AMERICAN AIRLINES
☎ 800/433-7300
www.aa.com
AMERICA WEST AIRLINES
☎ 800/235-9292
www.americawest.com
ATA AIRLINES
☎ 800/225-2995
www.ata.com

BRITISH AIRWAYS
☎ 800/247-9297
☎ 0870/850-9850 in the U.K.
www.british-airways.com
CONTINENTAL AIRLINES
☎ 800/525-0280
www.continental.com
DELTA AIR LINES
☎ 800/221-1212
www.delta.com
JETBLUE AIRWAYS
☎ 800/538-2583
www.jetblue.com
MIDWEST
☎ 800/452-2022
www.midwestexpress.com
NORTHWEST AIRLINES
☎ 800/225-2525
www.nwa.com
UNITED AIRLINES
☎ 800/241-6522
www.ual.com

US AIRWAYS
☎ 800/428-4322
www.usairways.com

VIRGIN ATLANTIC AIRWAYS
☎ 800/62-8621
☎ 0870/380-2007 in the U.K.
www.virgin-atlantic.com

Car-Rental Agencies

ALAMO
☎ 800/462-5266
www.alamo.com

AVIS
☎ 800/831-1212
www.avis.com

BUDGET
☎ 800/527-0700
www.budget.com

DOLLAR
☎ 800/800-3665
www.dollar.com

ENTERPRISE
☎ 800/261-7331
www.enterprise.com

HERTZ
☎ 800/654-3131
www.hertz.com

NATIONAL
☎ 800/227-7368
www.nationalcar.com

THRIFTY
☎ 800/847-4389
www.thrifty.com

Major Hotel & Motel Chains

BEST WESTERN INTERNATIONAL
☎ 800/780-7234
www.bestwestern.com

CLARION HOTELS
☎ 877/424-6423
www.choicehotels.com

COMFORT INN & SUITES
☎ 877/424-6423
www.choicehotels.com

COURTYARD BY MARRIOTT
☎ 800/321-2211
www.marriott.com

DAYS INN
☎ 800/329-7466
www.daysinn.com

DOUBLETREE HOTEL
☎ 800/222-8733
www.doubletree.com

FOUR SEASONS
☎ 800/819-5053
www.fourseasons.com

HAMPTON INN AND SUITES
☎ 800/426-7866
www.hamptoninn.com

HILTON HOTELS
☎ 800/445-8667
www.hilton.com

HOLIDAY INN
☎ 888/465-4329
www.holiday-inn.com

HOWARD JOHNSON
☎ 800/446-4656
www.hojo.com

HYATT HOTELS & RESORTS
☎ 888/591-1234
www.hyatt.com

INTERCONTINENTAL HOTELS & RESORTS
☎ 800/327-0200
www.intercontinental.com

MARRIOTT HOTELS
☎ 800/228-9290
www.marriott.com

OMNI
☎ 888/444-6664
www.omnihotels.com

RADISSON HOTELS INTERNATIONAL
☎ 888/201-1718
www.radisson.com

RAMADA INN
☎ 800/272-6232
www.ramada.com

RENAISSANCE
☎ 800/468-3571
www.marriott.com

RESIDENCE INN BY MARRIOTT
☎ 800/331-3131
www.marriott.com

RITZ-CARLTON
☎ 800/241-3333
www.ritzcarlton.com

SHERATON HOTELS & RESORTS
☎ 800/598-1753
www.starwoodhotels.com

WESTIN HOTELS & RESORTS
☎ 800/937-8461
www.starwoodhotels.com

WYNDHAM HOTELS & RESORTS
☎ 800/996-3426
www.wyndham.com

Index

See also Accommodations and Restaurant indexes, below.

Photo **Credits**

Explore over 3,500 destinations

TOKYO — 7766 miles
LONDON — 3818 miles
TORONTO — 4682 miles
SYDNEY — 5087 miles
NEW YORK — 4947 miles
LOS ANGELES — 2556 miles
HONG KONG — 5638 miles

Frommers.com makes it easy.

Find a destination. ✓ Book a trip. ✓ Get hot travel deals.
Buy a guidebook. ✓ Enter to win vacations. ✓ Listen to podcasts.
Check out the latest travel news. ✓ Share trip photos and memories.
And much more.

Frommers.com